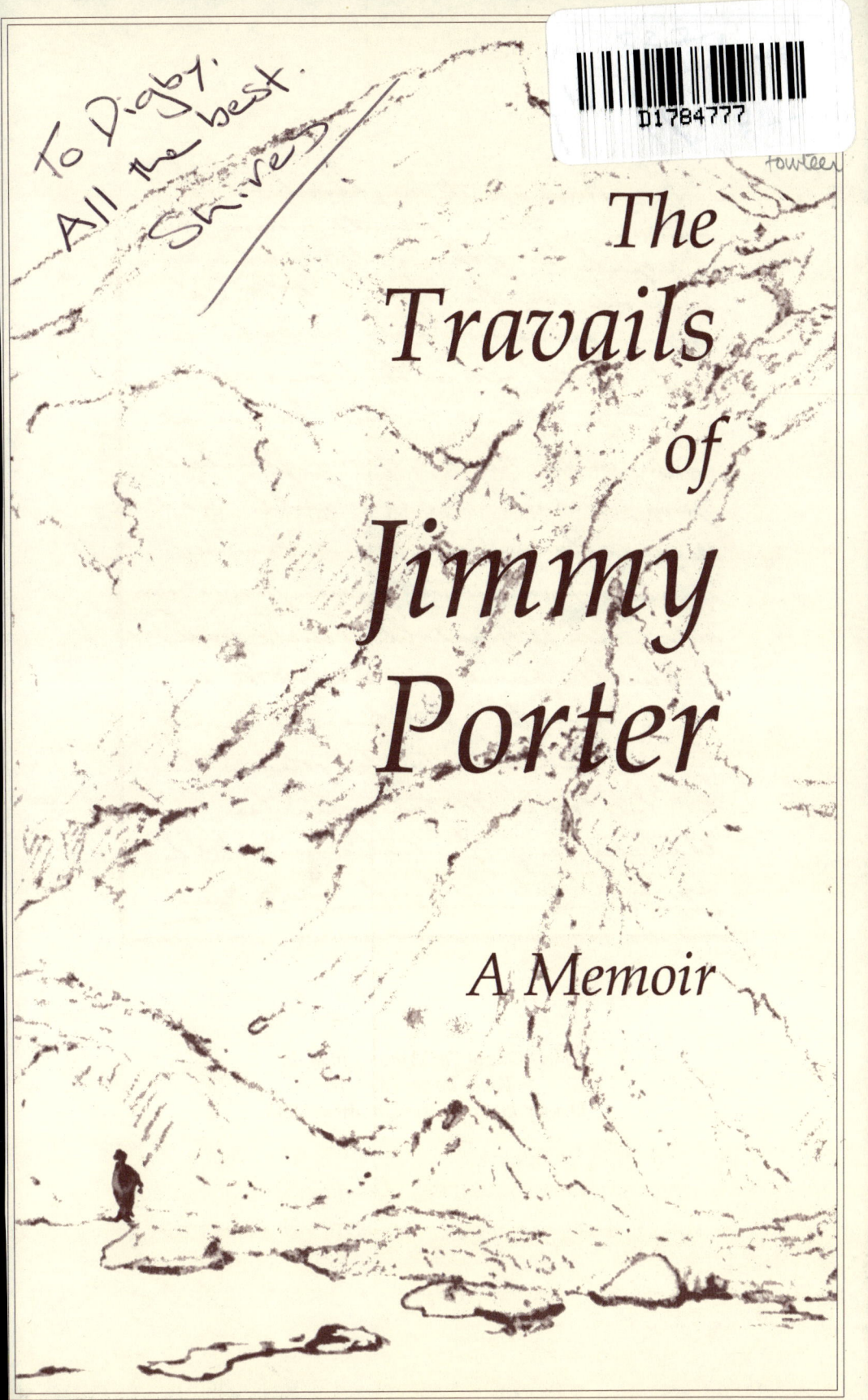

The
Travails
of
Jimmy
Porter

A Memoir

J.P. — Born in the neighbourhood of
London in 1807 — parents moving in
a respectable sphere of life — when 6
years old was transferred to the care
of my grandmother by her particular
request tho' not without great reluctance
on the part of my mother I remained
happy under the care of my grandmother
going to School regularly until I was
12 years of age) and whose kindness
you will find in the sequel proved my
ruin — at 12 years old I could write
a tolerable hand and was pretty forward
in Arithmetic: but being furnished
by my Schoolmaster for placing hair
in his cane so that when he
chastised any of us it would split
up and cut his hand, and indeed

Page One of the Manuscript of the
James Porter Memoir
Dixson Library State Library of NSW

The
Travails
of
Jimmy
Porter

A Memoir
1802 - 1842

Prepared for Publication by Richard Innes Davey
From the Original Manuscript by James Porter
And with an Afterword by Hamish Maxwell-Stewart

Published by The Round Earth Company
Strahan Tasmania

ACKNOWLEDGEMENTS

The Staff of the Mitchell and Dixson Library, Sydney
The Staff of the Tasmanian Heritage Collection
The Staff of the National Library
Hamish Maxwell-Stewart
Lucy Davey for background research
Stephen Dale for Handwriting Analysis
Printing Authority of Tasmania
and Kiah Rachel Davey for Technical Production

THE ILLUSTRATIONS

The Illustrations, held at the National Library, the Mitchell & Dixson Libraries State Library of NSW and the Tasmanian Heritage Collection, are by artists who were in the same places at the same time as James Porter: Thomas Scott in Hobart, Thomas Lempriere and Charles Costantini at Macquarie Harbour, Conrad Martens in Chile and Thomas Beagley Naylor on Norfolk Island.

Illustrations within the text.

Page 10:	Landscape~Conrad Martens	Dixson Library
Page 25:	Maria Island VDL~Thomas Scott	National Library
Page 32:	Lumber Yard~Thomas Lempriere	Tasmanian Heritage
Page 35:	Settlement Is MH~Thomas Lempriere	Tasmanian Heritage
Page 45:	Ship at Hells Gates~Charles Costantini	Tasmanian Heritage
Page 59:	Ox Cart~Conrad Martens	Dixson Library
Page 73:	Three Figures~Conrad Martens	Dixson Library
Page 107:	Norfolk Island~Thomas Beagley Naylor	National Library

First Printed by the Printing Authority of Tasmania 2003
Re-Printed 2011
ISBN 0-9750051-1-1

CONTENTS

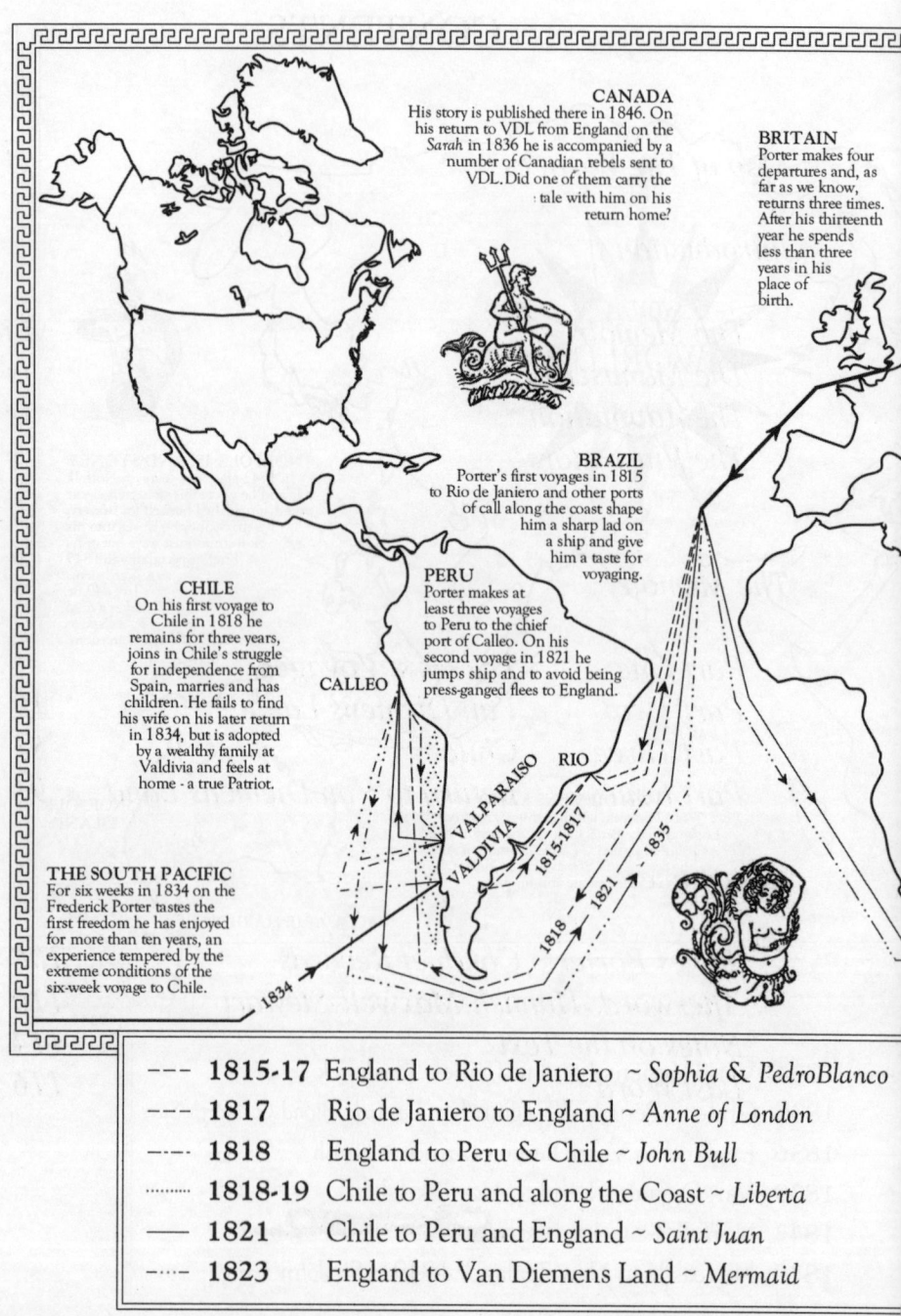

CANADA
His story is published there in 1846. On his return to VDL from England on the *Sarah* in 1836 he is accompanied by a number of Canadian rebels sent to VDL. Did one of them carry the : tale with him on his return home?

BRITAIN
Porter makes four departures and, as far as we know, returns three times. After his thirteenth year he spends less than three years in his place of birth.

BRAZIL
Porter's first voyages in 1815 to Rio de Janiero and other ports of call along the coast shape him a sharp lad on a ship and give him a taste for voyaging.

PERU
Porter makes at least three voyages to Peru to the chief port of Calleo. On his second voyage in 1821 he jumps ship and to avoid being press-ganged flees to England.

CHILE
On his first voyage to Chile in 1818 he remains for three years, joins in Chile's struggle for independence from Spain, marries and has children. He fails to find his wife on his later return in 1834, but is adopted by a wealthy family at Valdivia and feels at home - a true Patriot.

THE SOUTH PACIFIC
For six weeks in 1834 on the Frederick Porter tastes the first freedom he has enjoyed for more than ten years, an experience tempered by the extreme conditions of the six-week voyage to Chile.

CALLEO

VALPARAISO

VALDIVIA

RIO

1815-1817

1818

1821

1835

1834

---	1815-17	England to Rio de Janiero ~ *Sophia & PedroBlanco*
---	1817	Rio de Janiero to England ~ *Anne of London*
-·--	1818	England to Peru & Chile ~ *John Bull*
·········	1818-19	Chile to Peru and along the Coast ~ *Liberta*
——	1821	Chile to Peru and England ~ *Saint Juan*
-·--·	1823	England to Van Diemens Land ~ *Mermaid*

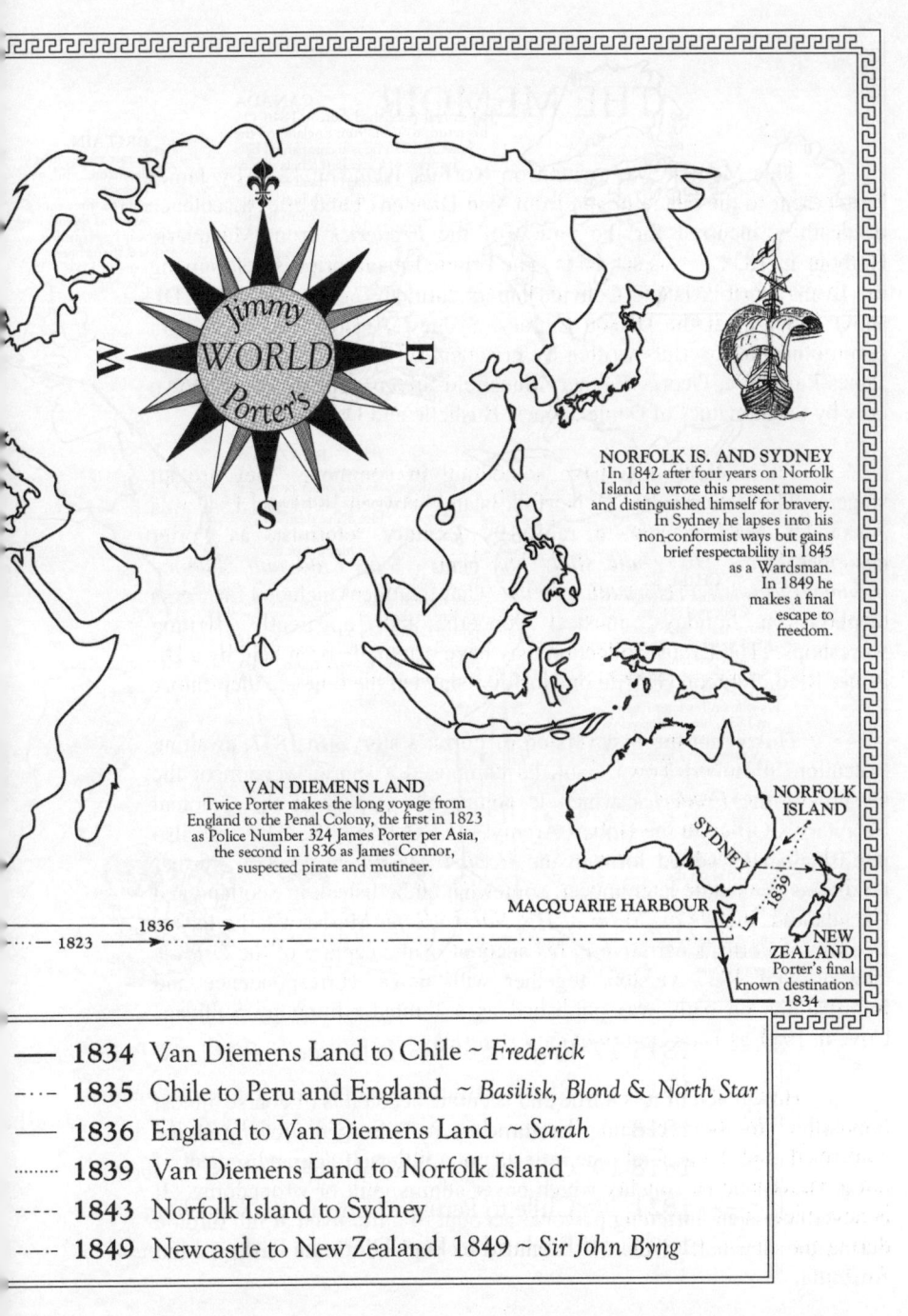

NORFOLK IS. AND SYDNEY
In 1842 after four years on Norfolk
Island he wrote this present memoir
and distinguished himself for bravery.
In Sydney he lapses into his
non-conformist ways but gains
brief respectability in 1845
as a Wardsman.
In 1849 he
makes a final
escape to
freedom.

VAN DIEMENS LAND
Twice Porter makes the long voyage from
England to the Penal Colony, the first in 1823
as Police Number 324 James Porter per Asia,
the second in 1836 as James Connor,
suspected pirate and mutineer.

NORFOLK
ISLAND

SYDNEY

1839

MACQUARIE HARBOUR

NEW
ZEALAND
Porter's final
known destination
1834

1836

1823

Jimmy
WORLD
Porter's

W

E

S

—— **1834** Van Diemens Land to Chile ~ *Frederick*

-·-· **1835** Chile to Peru and England ~ *Basilisk, Blond & North Star*

—— **1836** England to Van Diemens Land ~ *Sarah*

········ **1839** Van Diemens Land to Norfolk Island

----- **1843** Norfolk Island to Sydney

-··-·· **1849** Newcastle to New Zealand 1849 ~ *Sir John Byng*

THE MEMOIR

This Memoir was written on Norfolk Island in 1842 by James Porter, sent to the island prison from Van Diemens Land after a sentence of death - incurred for the piracy of the *Frederick* from Macquarie Harbour in 1834 - was set aside. The original manuscript is held among the Evans Norfolk Island Convict Papers entitled *The Ironed Gang* (DL MSQ 168 a-h) at the Dixson Library, Sydney, Australia, together with seven other manuscripts written by prisoners on Norfolk Island in 1842: James Lawrence, George Palmer, Mansfield Silverthorpe and four known only by the surnames of Daniel, Jones, Bushelle and Davies.

These eight men have something in common: they are all singers. The Commandant on Norfolk Island between 1840 and 1843 was Alexander MacConachie, a rare 19th Century reformist, as Porter describes him: *His whole study has been . . by Kind and Humane treatment to work a reformation in us.* That treatment included fireworks displays on holidays, musical concerts and, apparently, writing workshops. The Evans Collection may have originally been held by a Dr. James Ried, Surgeon General on Norfolk Island at the time . . . their tutor?

This is not the first version of Porter's story. In 1837, awaiting execution in Hobart Town Gaol, he composed a shorter version of the seizure of the *Frederick* which is among the papers of the Colonial Secretary's Office in the Hobart Archives (CSO 1/15339). This was also published in an edited form in the *Hobart Almanack* of 1838. Further renditions of the tale later appear, somewhat embellished, in Scotland and Canada and, in *For the Term of His Natural Life*, Marcus Clarke makes free use of Porter's narrative in his account of the capture of the *Osprey*. The original 1837 version, together with notes, correspondence and informations on oath, was published as a limited edition by Sullivans Cove in 1981 as *The Capture of the Frederick*.

How much of it is a true and accurate account is of course almost impossible to say: certain inaccuracies and exaggerations can be confirmed, and the general tone reflects not a little self-aggrandisement, if not a narcissistic personality which never admits guilt or wrongdoing. It is nevertheless an intriguing personal account of a life lived at full throttle during the first half of the 19th Century in England, South America and Australia.

THE MANUSCRIPT

The manuscript is written in several hands - the two pages reproduced (pp ii and 90) are clearly different, and at times the writing becomes larger and naively formed (above), but the signature at the end is quite bold and confident. The style of punctuation changes markedly in the later sections, with less use of the dash rather than stops or commas, perhaps indicating that the first half or more of the manuscript was dictated, the style reflecting a manner of speech and storytelling.

Results of an examination of photocopies of the 140 pages in the Norfolk Island Manuscript by a forensic document examiner, Stephen Dale, indicate that there are three writers: pages 1-4 and 9-80 in the same hand, a second writer pages 5-8 only, and a third writer pages 81-140 who would seem to be Porter himself, being consistent with the signature. None of these hands correspond to the handwriting of the other seven Norfolk Island writers, each of which is distinct from the each of the others. The handwriting in the earlier 1837 manuscript in Hobart matches none of the hands in the Norfolk Island work: it is a neat, copybook hand throughout the document, which is quite likely to be a clerk's copy of what may have been a very rough and scratchy original.

ADAPTATION

The manuscript is 140 pages, continuous, without chapters, sections or paragraph breaks, making the narrative a rather breathless read. In translating the manuscript to print the narrative is divided into four parts, sectioned to allow the reader to pause occasionally, brief narrative headings added, and some adjustments made to aid a smooth reading of text while maintaining a feeling for the original.

Porter's *spelling*, or that of his scribes, has been reproduced as it appears, except in a very few instances where a misspelling actually distorts the sense. Porter's *punctuation* has been substantially maintained, but stops added as required, of which there are very few in the original. *Upper case* is reproduced as used, although that is not always clear in the writing. Words and some phrases are frequently *underlined*: in adapting *italics* are used. The *ampersand* (&) is used as it appears in the manuscript, but frequent *abbreviations* (Capt., W^m. and others) are reproduced in full. Several words are added in [square brackets] where the sense demands it.

THE ILLUSTRATORS

Conrad Martens ~ Martens left England in 1833 as an artist aboard the *Hyacinth* but the expedition failed and Martens was stranded in Rio de Janiero. He then joined the *Beagle* from November 1833 to July 1834, and was therefore sketching in Chile near Valparaiso when the *Frederick* escapees arrived in nearby Valdivia. He later established himself as a landscape artist in Sydney Australia.

Thomas Scott ~ Born in Scotland and trained as a surveyor, he came to VDL in 1821 and was appointed Assistant Surveyor to G.W.Evans. He sketched throughout VDL but particularly on the East Coast. Passed over for the post as Surveyor General, he left the colony in 1834.

Thomas Lempriere ~ Commissariat Officer at Macquarie Harbour in the years when James Porter was there, and later at Port Arthur. He wrote an account of the Penal Settlements in VDL and his sketchbooks held at the Allport Museum in Hobart offer rare detail of life in these settlements.

Charles Henri Theodore Costantini ~ A French artist sent to VDL from England for paying too ardent attention to a gentleman's wife, then to Macquarie Harbour for forgery. Lempriere employed him as an artist to record the Settlement, and at least some of the work attributed to Lempriere bears the hallmarks of Costantini.

Rev. Thomas Beagley Naylor ~ Chaplain on Norfolk Island 1838-45 who reluctantly became a convert to the reformist approach of Alexander McConachie. As Porter was a skilled sailor he may have been among those sketched waiting to dock the vessel arriving on Norfolk Island in 1842 - the same year in which this memoir was written.

x

PART ONE

The First Voyages

1802-1822

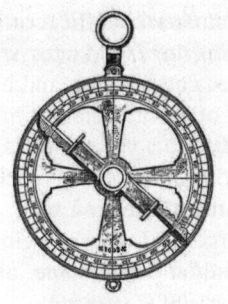

The Interior of the
Theatre Royal Drury Lane
at the time of its Restoration
1812-1813

About this time the young James Porter
'takes french leave to go to the
theatre at Drury Lane'.

Published in 'La Belle Assemblee' Vol 6, 1813
Possibly a sketch by
Benjamin Dean Wyatt
Architect of the Theatre Restoration

Courtesy of the Hector Berlioz website
(www.hberlioz.com)

PART ONE

The First Voyages

1802-1822

Born in the neighbourhood of London in 1802 — parents moving in a respectable sphere of life — when six years old I was transferred to the care of my grandmother by her particular request, tho' not without great reluctance on the part of my mother. I remained happy under the care of my grandmother (going to school regularly until I was 12 years of age) and whose kindness you will find in the Sequel proved my ruin — at 12 years old I could write a tolerable hand and was pretty forward in arithmetic: but being punished by my schoolmaster for placing hair in his cane so that when he chastised any of us it would split up and cut his hand, and indeed to this day and through all my misfortunes and rambles the same propensity for mischief haunts me.

I took a great dislike to him and all kind of scholastic duties, continually playing the truant, which to my sorrow — I was not sufficiently checked by my grandmother, and my schoolmaster was *too* severe, beating *out* one devil and beating *in* two. I was at last determined to tell my grandmother that I totally disliked my schoolmaster, and persuaded her to let me remain at home entirely. Time passed merrily with me then — no one controlled me — playing about with neighbours' children about my own age I soon got initiated into vice — I took french leave one night and went to the Drury Lane Theatre — plundering my grandmother to support my villainous extravagances, which has caused many a sad and solitary hour to my doating relative and finally hurried her to her grave. This I saw, and *had heart* then to sue for pardon, declaring I would not steal any more nor cause her any more uneasiness — had I then been separated from my acquaintances and sent to sea under good treatment — in a man o' war it would have cured all.

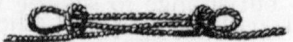

Things went on well for a short time yet I could not get the thoughts of the Theatre out of my head and was determined to see it again and how to obtain the means? My pals, two boys about my own age spotted a gentleman's house and asked me if I would go into the parlour window at dusk (sneaking) and take a timepiece off the mantlepiece which I did — they receiving the booty and (fencing) selling it — giving me little or nothing of the amount of it. I being the only person seen about the house was apprehended and taken to my grandmother who swooned away. My parents were sent for and the gentleman would not prosecute on the account of the respectability of my parents; but persuaded them to send me to sea.

Everything was got ready for me that I should require on my passage from London to Gravesend as my friends had come to a determination that I should go to my Uncle that resided there, having two vessels of his own, a Brig and Schooner. However, the day arrived that I embarked having a good fit out, and in the afternoon at 4 o'clock I landed in Gravesend my relations being there ready to receive me. It was the first time I ever saw my Uncle in my life and I do assure you I did not like his stern features, nor the reception I met with. I wish merely to give you an outline of my Uncle's character, he was a man inured to hardship at sea, and had lost vessel after vessel, by having on board contraband goods, but being indefatigable in his pursuit of smuggling he proved fortunate in the long run, and at the time I went to live with him he was independent – but strange to say, he was so partial to the French Coast where he had accumulated so much wealth that he could not avoid acting the part (on board his Schooner) of a *Contrabandista*. This was the precise character of the Uncle and man I had to deal with, with his bronzed features and stern countenance he thus addressed me:

Well, Nephew, or rather land shark, I find by a letter I have received you have been making too free with your can hooks (a phrase used by seamen, meaning my hands) *in taking that which does not belong to you and by those means hastening the death of your*

5

grandmother that watched over you in your childhood. However I shall say no more to you about it at present for I mean to send you on two or three voyages in my Brig the Sophia command by a skipper that will either make a sailor of you or an idiot by giving you a dry starting once or twice a day (with a self point) to keep the scurvy out of your bones.

My Aunt rebuked him several times for being so harsh with me that it may be the cause of my running away and proving my ruin. By this time we reached his dwelling the distance of two miles from where I landed and a most splendid little place it was, being entwined with ground hivey and a beautiful garden both front and back. The appearance of this pleasant spot caused me to forget, in a great measure, the harsh reception I met from my stern Uncle. I had a little conversation the same evening with my Aunt whose kindness to me alleviated that pang which my Uncle [caused] through his (as I considered) harsh treatment towards me on my first landing. She informed me likewise that my Cousin was expected home every day, having command of the schooner.

My cousin returned from his voyage in the year 1815, it was the first time I ever seen him, he was then only 20 years old. He proved very kind to me at first, until he got acquainted with my dishonesty which caused him to turn distant to me. This was worse to my feelings, young as I was, than any punishment could have been. I was determined to make my exit as soon as possible but before I could, I was hurried on board my Uncle's Brig bound for Rio de Janeira. In a few days after I was took leave of my Uncle and Cousin and being at that time pleased with my new situation.

In the course of a little time, having favorable breeze, we were in Blue Water. It was not until then that I felt the cruel hands of Captain Lindsey and before I hardly knew what a ship was, I was mastheaded on the most trivial occasion, where I was obliged to hold on like grim death to a topmast backstay, and worse than all we made very bad weather and a long passage, tho' it was the means of making a sharp lad of me. We reached the port of our destination and on the Saturday we brought up before the town by evening. I went on shore with the Captain and I did not like the place owing to seeing so many Negro Slaves and I was determined if possible to run away from the Brig on account of the Captain's cruelty towards me, tho' he pretended to be kind to me again.

The next day being Sunday I was walking the deck studying how I could escape knowing that I was an entire stranger to the place, the language or customs of the people, when a Seaman named Mr. Huntington called me to the forecastle. We conversed about our grievances, and he sounded me, pushing me to make a complaint to my Uncle concerning the Captain's ill treatment of me on the voyage. I hesitated before I told him that I thought my uncle must have given such orders to the Captain to use me as he thought proper, and under those considerations I never wished to see either Uncle or Captain any more, and that rather than I would go back with him again I would throw myself overboard which would end my misfortunes. He said if such was my determination — and as I was kind to the men in the forecastle — if I liked he would get a vessel for himself & me, we should both leave together — I gave my consent and thanked him for his kindness.

After an hour he got permission to go on shore and about 4 o'clock he returned on board. He called me to him & informed me that he had a vessel for us both that was bound for Rio Plata and that I must get what little things I had belonging to me by 9 or 10 o'clock that night — I was elevated at the thoughts of it and went down to the cabin. The Mate was drunk & I passed about unnoticed, brought my clothing up one by one, put them into my clothes bag & concealed them until night. I also took 50 dubloons and a hundred dollars belonging to the Captain, to defray expenses — this I did not mention to my shipmate. Nine o'clock came, my friend and me being in the Anchor Watch, two men and a boy — the jolly boat came along side. I was also on the alert, I handed the Clothing down to my friend but the Money I concealed on my person.

We got into her and shoved off and I thought it was the happiest moment of my life. A few strokes brought us alongside of a schooner, we got on deck in silence & proceeded to the forecastle where there was plenty of everything, and the next morning at 8 o'clock we had cleared the outer fort and was in a fair way for our destined port. The Captain's name was Pedro Blanco a very keen fellow, he had formerly been Captain of a Slaver. My friend being an able seaman received 16 dollars and small stores and the Captain said that if I made myself handy he would give me 12 dollars per month.

I was content and remained with him for upwards of a 12 month, making several voyages with him, never caring much about going ashore until I had learned some of the language. However myself & friend left the schooner and shipped in a Barque named the *Anne of London* homeward bound from Rio. We received very good usage on board.

It was the latter end of the year 1815 when I first left England, and when I landed in England again it was the end of 1817. I made the best of my way to London with my friend (who still remained with me) to my friends whom I found well, & was rather surprised at seeing me for they had mourned me as dead. I gave them an explicit account of my treatment at my Uncle's and also the cruelty practiced on me on board my Uncle's brig the *Sophia*, and that I was certain my Uncle had given him orders to that effect that I should be harshly dealt with. This caused harsh words between my father and Uncle — and it took a long time before they were friends, being brothers — but in the course of time all things were amicably settled.

I remained at home a few months when I again longed to be at sea. I then shipped aboard a whaler named the *John Bull* belonging to Bennett & Co. for a three years voyage in the Sperm fishery off the coast of Peru. This was in 1818 — I took leave of my Parents, Sisters & Brothers — whom I could not erase from my memory.

The First Voyages

I was at this time a smart lad in a ship. We had a good passage until we neared the Horn — terrific seas and dreadful colds— icicles & Ice Bergs: I never experienced any real hardship until now, the cold being almost unsupportable. We were compelled to keep Man o' War watches for fear of the Ice — several of the crew were injured by the cold and it caused one man's death — the only serious misfortune that happened.

Shortly after we doubled the Cape we got into fine weather: feeling the warm effect of the Bengal Blanket (the Sun) aloft, we lowered the boats several times and had good luck in fishing. We remained six months cruising about, put into Valparaiso to refresh ship. I swayed away (drew large) on the slop chest, and the second day, having all I wanted on shore and having a good bit of money about me, I bid farewell to the Ship, and a Spanish girl stowed me away on her father's premises until the ship sailed again. I then hove in sight to the satisfaction of the young Patriot and her friends. Her father's name was Fernando Martel, her own name Narcissus. I began to think of marriage by the continual persuasion of her friends — I considered myself too young, I was then only sixteen. I told her father I would make a voyage or two and then I would consent — this he agreed to, and I shipped in the *Liberta*, an armed schooner to take troops and land them in different parts of the Coast. This was about the time Lord Cochrane had the three Polacres fighting on behalf of the South Americans; my wages was 18 dollars a month as I was termed a European. There were several of my Countrymen on Board, tho' the greatest part of the crew were Cholers or Creoles — a brave race of men, very swarthy, their Fathers were Spanish & Mothers native Americans.

I remained in the *Liberta* for twelve months, sometimes skirmishing ashore, & otherwise giving the Spaniards a round turn from the schooner from our two Long Toms. It was about 14 months before I returned to my friend Fernando Martel. I now considered myself fit for any hardship — I met with a very kind reception as if I was their own child, and in a short time Narcissa and myself were united in wedlock.

Now commenced a scene of misery & trouble.

After our marriage festival which lasted three days — a custom in that country — it was the request of my father and mother in law that I should not go to sea any more but that I should live in an extensive farm which became my own property at the marriage. I agreed to the proposal and myself & wife's friends got underweigh the next day for the farm which was situated

11

twenty one miles on the road to St Iago. I found it a most beautiful spot quite congenial to my feelings and I remained happy in the new situation for upwards of two years — my wife had a boy and a girl during this time — the girl died shortly after its birth. The country was very much agitated this time as the patriots were contending for their independence and Lord Cochrane was very busy along the coast — scarce a man could call his life his own without being on the alert. I again (like Gulliver) felt an inclination to go to sea for a trip or two and mentioned it to my wife which gave her great uneasiness, but having seen her Parents, with great persuasion, they consented.

After taking an affectionate leave of my Wife and Son, I shipped on a Chilean Brig called the *Saint Juan* bound to Calleo in Peru. Our Captain was a Swede named Frederick Simpson. As soon as we brought up he went to Lima for a few days — when I found out the Brig was on a contraband voyage, which did not suit me at that time, and on that account was determined to leave her, and before the Captain returned from Lima I went on shore with french leave. When the military were sent in pursuit of me & found me in a grog shop, the chief mate being with them pointed me out — I, being rather groggy with *aquadent*, would not go with them — they commenced using their sabres by order of the Mate. I then drew a Sling Shot out of my pocket to defend myself with and a regular engagement occurred — there being a couple of Blue

Jackets in the Grog Shop with me, assisted me against the four. The Chief mate drew one of his country knives on me — he being a Frenchman. Finding I had no other alternative but to fight or lose my life I let drive my sling shot and struck the mate on the back of the head — at that moment he was about stabbing me with his knife — I bilged in his head gear with the blow & he fell senseless at my feet; the two sailors that were there with me played their part and knocked down two soldiers out of the three, when the other bolted — I received a slight wound in the head and one of the sailors got a severe gash in the arm — however we were compelled to make our escape as quick as possible for we expected a reinforcement in pursuit of us.

The two sailors made the best of their way to their respective ships when I took the back until evening & then came down the back to the sea side. I then returned to the Grog Shop where the fray took place when I heard some soldiers carousing; I watched my opportunity and beckoned to a seaman, he came to me: I related the whole of the circumstances — he informed me the men who assisted me were his shipmates belonging to the *Mermaid* Barque and they were due to sail next day for England. I asked if they were in want of hands, replied *Yes* and that it would be better for me to ship as quickly as possible — that the man I had struck with the shot was dead, his skull being fractured, & it was twenty to one if they caught me that I should be shot for it.

I was aware of this and took his advice — he called his shipmates out (five in number) and they consented to go on board with me. On our way to the ship I took them to the house where I left my things that I brought on shore — I went in for them but they refused giving them saying I was the man who ran away from the brig — I insisted on having them, a row ensued, when the seamen came in and we *rushed* for them & compelled them to give them up against their will. We then made the best of our way on board of the Barque & went down to the forecastle until morning, when Captain Welsh willingly shipped me — for I told him the truth and hid nothing of the proceedings.

That morning at 11 o'clock we bid farewell to the Half Moon Battery with a Stiff Breeze in our favour. It was not until the next day that I was stung with *remorse* at the very idea of leaving my wife & child behind me, yet I hoped I should see them once again — my life was rather miserable, but in the course of a fortnight or three weeks I felt a little easier in my mind and was determined that, should I reach England in safety, after having an interview with my friends, I would immediately ship for Valparaiso, consider it my native land, there to rest happy with my wife and child. Buoyed up with fresh hopes I let nothing trouble me, not thinking, alas, I had taken my leave of them for ever — painful it was to me and ever will be the sad reflection, having brought it all upon myself by being too hasty — my mind will not allow me to comment upon this.

After a stormy passage I landed once more in my native land, tho' not with that pleasure I formerly had done. I received my wages and made the best of my way to my friends whom I found all well & happy to receive me, it being the latter part of the year 1821. I informed my friends that I was married in South

America & that I had a Son living and that I would return very shortly never to part from them more, unless I brought them home with me — they could not say wrong to this — as they seen my feelings were strong on the subject.

I remained at home until 1822 when getting acquainted with loose company & money being short I was persuaded to make one push which would make me rich or cost me my life. I agreed to it and should I succeed, to go to Liverpool and ship for South America.

I went with two more men & in the dead of night went on board of a Cutter at anchor off Northfleet, secured the men on board and took a great quantity of Silk and Beaver which was of great value (to hatters I suspect?). We reached London in safety — but one of the thieves concealed a quantity of Silk and Beaver about his person without our knowledge with a view to *putting us in the hole* (defrauding us) for part of the Booty — he was apprehended & he then betrayed me and the other man. We were put in prison, found guilty — & condemned to die.

It was my determination not to let my parents know anything of my dishonesty or disgraceful death for I expected nothing else — but the villain that had betrayed us was not satisfied with the injury he had done me, but he went to my parents and told them all the particulars — the shock nearly cost my mother her life — but being of strong constitution she recovered. Not so my grandmother, the shock was more than she could bear — and before the news came that I was reprieved she died — my name being the last words she pronounced. A few days after this I was sent to the hulks where the Work and Usage made me often contemplate Suicide — and nothing but the hope of soon getting away could induce me to remain in that dreadful place.

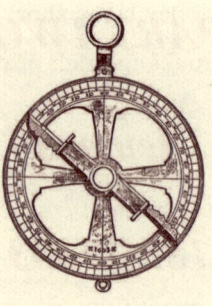

End Part One

PART TWO

Van Diemens Land

1823-1833

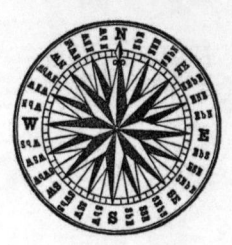

Sketch of Hobart by Thomas Scott 1826
Mitchell Library State Library of NSW

PART TWO

Van Diemens Land

1823—1833

I was forwarded to Van Diemens Land in the ship *Asia* with 249 other unfortunates & shortly after getting on board we were favoured with a fine wind & in the course of a few days we were out of sight of land. The Captain released me out of irons, sooner than most of the other prisoners & I helped to work ship, being allowed the ration and grog of a seaman. Nothing of any consequence happened until we came in sight of the Cape of Good Hope, where we were taken aback with studding sails low & aloft, in consequence of the man at the helm nodding — the quick command of the Captain and the activity of the crew soon put all to right — and from that time every thing went on well

19

and we arrived safe at Van Diemens Land & came to an anchor opposite the Battery of Hobart Town after a voyage of 4 months & 2 days.

After our arrival we were detained in harbour a few days, were then landed & sent to Gaol — to wait until we were disposed of to our Masters. I being a Mariner and no tradesman therefore I expected to get a bad Master (a *Dungaree Settler* — to work from sun to sun on short commons). A fellow prisoner, a Jew, told me to hail for a White Smith & that I would get a good master by that means, and also stay in town (a great desire of *all prisoners*). I agreed to this but I told the Jew to inform the Emigrant that I was a good tradesman, but if he came to ask me that I was sure to deny my trade as I did not intend to work at it any more if I could avoid it. This contrivance succeeded — the Master came and asked me if I was a Smith and I said *No*. He replied *Never mind I'll chance you. I can tell by your looks you are a tradesman,* & immediately got me booked to him. I went home with him, his name was Mr. Pulling. I done no work that day but the next morning I was conducted into the Blacksmith's shop where his other man was getting a Welding Heat ready: as soon as it came out of the fire Mr. Pulling ordered me to be ready to strike with a 14 pound sledge hammer. I told him *again* I knew nothing about such work, he requested me not to be *too* stubborn — however to satisfy him I gave him a few blows, when he was *quite* satisfied — I had told him the truth, he not perceiving the cheat, and on that account he would not turn me into Government employ, but said I must do the best I could for him about the house.

20

I did so, and remained with him until he failed in business and was much reduced — I thought I ought to assist him in return for his kindness to me for I was very sorry to see his children in want — I could not get what I wanted by work (labouring — as I had no trade) but I was determined to obtain it by fair or foul means — for my poor Master had taken it so much to heart that he appeared deranged.

Therefore in the evening I took a small Dinghy (a *very small* sort of boat or Canoe) out of the creek, watched my opportunity and got alongside of the Barque *Bengal Merchant* — I soon made my way to the Cabins and brought away a bag containing upwards of 300 sovereigns besides a quantity of loose silver which I put into my pockets, and then returning on deck (it being dark) I met a man which proved to be the Steward — he was so much astonished that he gave me an opportunity of pushing him down on the deck before he could give an alarm.

By this time I was in the Mizzen chains and the dinghy having gone adrift there was no other alternative but to go overboard or be caught *& hanged*. I then took to the water. I found the weight of the money *&* clothing was a great incumberance — there was a great outcry from ship to ship. I made the best of my way to a Buoy which found answered all my wishes. I hung on there and when I found boats approaching me I hauled myself under water and remained as long as I could until I supposed they had passed — if not I kept my head close to the Buoy level with the water — I escaped their search and got safe ashore with my cargo.

I made the best of my way home to my Mistress &
Children whom I found crying — it was late at night before I got
home. She seen I was wet and then very cold. She asked me how I
came so wet — I told her not to tell any person what she saw or it
would surely cost me my life — I told her the reason I did it — she
cried & it was a long time before I could pacify her. I slept little
that night & early in the morning I bought a plentiful supply of
food for the house in different shops — enough for six months — I
gave her some money and told her to turn me in to Government
Service, so that if I was *pulled* (taken for a crime of any sort) she
would not be suspected of having a knowledge of the robbery —
she at length consented and next day I was turned into Barracks —
there was a £100 reward (& a free pardon) to any *prisone*r that
would give information of the robbery. I had only been in
Government but three days before Mr Pulling (my late Master)
came home and finding things strangely altered he asked his wife
how it came. She informed him I had bought it and it was my own
request to go into Barracks — this caused some suspicion — he
came to me and asked me where I got the money. I did not fancy
this — I said it was none of his [business] — he took the affront at
this and left me in a surly mood.

I began to suspect something serious might happen & I
was rather uneasy and the next day my mistress came to me,
crying, telling me to make my escape for she thought her husband
meant to do me an injury & had found two sovereigns I had given
her & he hinted about the reward & robbery of the Barque. I asked
her if she said any thing — she said she would die first — I was

quite satisfied — and as she was going away, up came her husband & looked at me but did not speak. I understood his meaning — he was jealous (without cause). *One hour* afterwards I was apprehended for the robbery but had nothing about me to lead to suspicion. I was brought before the Magistrate (a feeling Gentleman — *rare* to be found in these Colonies). The Captain & the Steward made their appearance but could not identify me, and the Magistrate gave my late Master a severe reprimand for his ingratitude to me, for I told the Magistrate I brought money from home which squared the yards every way.

In a few days after I was a pulling hand in the Governor's Barge & was afterwards made Coxswain of the Secretary's Gig, and at this time the Natives (aborigines) were killing the white people whenever they fell in with them. All things went well for a few months until orders came down from Governor Arthur that a Whale Boat was to be manned directly to take dispatches to Maria Island, as no vessel was to be procured — and at any time in cases of emergency a Sailing Vessel was uncertain — the boat was manned. The other Coxswain being absent on duty it came to my lot to take charge of the boat — with strict orders (caution) how I crossed East Bay neck — the most ferocious and daring blacks (the Stony Creek Tribe). I was allowed to take firearms, cutlasses etc for the protection of ourselves. I had a blunderbuss that Captain Welsh lent me (he was Superintendent of Government Craft).

23

Van Diemens Land

We run with a lug sail at the rate of 7 knots per hour. Towards dusk we made the neck of land we had to cross. As we neared the beach I could see the Blacks' fires & ordered the men to get out as quiet as possible & we succeeded in hauling the boat about two thirds across before we were disturbed — the distance to haul her is near a mile. A dog belonging to the Blacks was hunting opossums and set up a howl the moment he saw us, which alarmed the natives. They came to the spot some with firebrands & more with their war implements. I ordered the men to seize their fire arms — the moment we got our muskets they let drive a shower of spears at us at random — one of them struck the bowman in the fleshy part of the arm. We rushed upon them & fired our pistols at them, they all fled — we then got to the boat and dragged her over the Neck — but before we could launch her another shower of spears fell among us. We were in such a hurry to get her launched that we did not properly know who was injured — but I was soon informed that the bowman was killed — a spear went through his intestines & he never spoke more.

This left me a hand short — and now was the most difficult part of the passage. The channel where I was compelled to take the Boat through was overhung by a Bluff Point where the natives could stand and kill every man of us with spears and stones. I could not near the surf, which compelled me to wait till morning. At daylight we pulled for the sea gate, when we seen a number of Blacks waiting for us — they would have been able to wade to the boat and surround us (as it was low water). I told the crew to strip to their trowsers and was determined to take the East

Spit — dreadful surf — but our only chance to escape the natives. As we neared the surf the Blacks gave a yell — I told the men not to mind it but mind their duty — we shipped about 50 gallons of water. We cleared our danger owing entirely to the steady manner the men done their duty.

We made Maria Island that night — when we arrived at the Island I took the dispatches to the Commandant, Major Lord — took the body out of the boat to the Hospital. I informed the Major what happened & that I should require another hand, our muskets cleaned, more powder, swan shot & ball cartridge. I got what I wanted, buried the man — got my dispatches and prepared to return, determined to give the Blacks a warm reception if we were compelled to go that passage. We took our departure at daylight for Hobart Town, but the wind blowing at S.W. I could not think of doubling Cape Pillar, so in the evening with the oars muffled, shot her quietly through the sea gate.

We experienced so much danger we could see the fires of the Blacks in shore — the darkness of the night sheltered us from their view and in an hour after we entered the sea gate we made the spot where we had to drag the boat across — it was silent as the grave, not a ripple on the water. I ordered the crew to look to their firearms & see that all was ready at a moment's notice — we took a gill of grog each for we were determined to pull the boat across the neck as quick as possible, otherwise, to have waited for the morning, we should have been surrounded by the Blacks & no doubt some of us (if not all) lose our lives.

Everything being ready we commenced our dangerous task — we had got the boat on end as near as possible when about 200 yards we heard a distant shout — we proceeded almost half way when we came across some of their fires in our very track. I proposed that we should keep watch and watch over the boat during the night, in hopes if the savages did not already see us that they would go off before morning — this succeeded, for in the morning the Blacks went off hunting and fishing. When we got within a short distance of the place we had to launch her we heard the barking of dogs — we lay in ambush for a little time, and presently up came a large kangaroo followed by two large dogs and shortly after four native Blacks — they immediately came to the boat and began to plunder her of every thing portable, when we rushed on them with our cutlasses & dispatched the four. When we came towards the beach we found it covered with Blacks, and our only hope was to rush the boat through them to the water, and so quick was our movements and so well did the men perform their duty that we got her two thirds in the water before they recovered from their astonishment. We had great difficulty in getting the boat launched & it was not without firing at the Blacks that we succeeded finally in getting away — they waded after us and several of their spears stuck in the whale boat — we killed their Chief.

In a few hours made Elizabeth Island and catching a breeze from the E.S.E. we stretched out for Hobart Town, which we reached in safety — I took the dispatches to Governor Arthur. The Boat's Crew were ordered a Ticket of Leave after six month's good conduct — I got charge of the *Rambler* Cutter of 48 tons & gave every satisfaction. I was earning plenty of money, not being addicted to drinking. Some Scoundrels gave information that I was going to take away the Cutter — this caused the first suspicion of my character and the cause of my misery. I was not looked upon as a person trustworthy, therefore I was determined to make my escape from the Colony as soon as I could get a chance.

The *Elizabeth* Brig was lying at Bricks' Bay 30 miles from town, & myself and a young man named Thomas Rush took a Lug Sail out of the sail loft, swam to a whale boat at her moorings, cut her away and made our way to the Brig & shipped in her. She was bound to Macquarie Islands for Elephant oil, a very dangerous voyage — the Brig got under way but could not weather the point of the bay. The wind being scant we brought up again & that night I was taken prisoner, tried for taking the whale boat, but in consequence of a good character from Captain Welsh and other gentlemen, I was acquitted and in a few days got charge of a schooner of 25 tons.

Van Diemens Land

There were two more men attached to her — one of the hands being nearly free stole some pine plank to make himself a sea chest and took it on board without my knowledge. I was on shore at the time — he was taken to gaol for it, and me having charge of the schooner I was apprehended — the man only wanted ten days to do out of 14 years, he was nearly broken-hearted and asked if there was any chance of his being saved — I said none, except for me to take it on myself. I consented to get convicted if he would promise to have a whaleboat ready when I got sent to a Chain Gang for me to abscond & run down into the Straights with. He promised me he would — I consented, acquitted him, & convicted myself by acknowledging to the planks — I got 7 years transportation.

I was not downcast at this for I depended on the Whale Boat — I went to the Chain Gang and one of the most dreadful places I ever seen. I preferred death to remaining there three years — and the ungrateful wretch whom I thus sacrificed myself for never came near me. I was determined to escape from this scene of wretchedness or perish in the attempt. I wanted to collect a crew for a whale boat. I put the question to them, they agreed, and the Saturday came we were to seize the sentry and overseers & fly from slavery — I could find that my new companions were not the stuff I took them for, as they wished me to risk all and them nothing. I was aware of my situation, my irons being cut — so I went up to the sentry, pushed him off the bank and ran as quick as possible — my pursuers were following. I had just sufficient time to lash the rings of the irons to each leg — my only plan was to plunge into the river. I did so & none followed me. I got to a place called Bedlam Wales — I seen a boat coming after me & went further down the river side & swam back again — when I got on the shore I went into the town, crossed at the back of Government House. I was recognized & a fresh pursuit. Night came on & I managed to get to the house of Mr Mansfield who was Pilot — he asked me where I was going. I told him after the *Rambler* Cutter which had sailed without me & I expected to find her at anchor in Sandy Bay.

He ordered me supper and to sleep at his house that night — I could not pull my trousers off on account of the irons. I told the people in the house to call me early. One of the youths I slept with in his house felt one of my irons in the course of the night. He acquainted his brother who got up and struck a light — they found all as it was. I told them the truth, they pitied me & said they would not tell their father & for me to sleep & they would keep good watch for me, & loose the Mastiff dog, so that no person could approach without notice. I soon fell into a sound sleep — I got up at day dawn, took my leave of my two kind young protectors.

I made the best of my way to the Signal Mount where there were two men — one of them I knew, he also knew my situation. He wanted to take me prisoner, he took a musket — I took an axe & before he could level his piece at me I brought him to the ground with a blow of the pole of the axe. I had a great mind to settle him, but got the better of my passion & left him on the ground — on leaving the hut I saw the other man coming with the water. I escaped his notice & went on my journey for Oyster Bay with the hope of getting a dinghy to cross to Bruny Island. However I lost myself for three days in the Bush without a morsel of food. It was then I felt the horrors of famishing. On the fourth morning I was aroused by a dog barking in pursuit of kangaroo. I soon seen two dogs killing a kangaroo not 50 yards from me — I expected to see the owner but he did not appear, so I took a hearty meal of the raw flesh and blood of the kangaroo. It was refreshing though insipid repast.

I then started afresh on my journey and towards evening reached the head of Little Oyster bay, where two men were lime burning. I went to the Hut to remain until morning when I found an opportunity of breaking my irons off my legs which was a happy releasement. As soon as daylight appeared I went to the waterside in hopes of stealing a Dinghy to get across to Bruny Island, when a party of police made their appearance: I concealed myself until an opportunity served and then I rushed into the limeburners' boat to take me across the river — the Police seen me, ran down and commenced a sharp fire at me — I escaped, and got across to the Island to Blubbers Bay where there was a vessel taking in oil, and when her cargo was on board (for London direct), I tried all I could to get on board but the weather set in so bad from the S.E. that it was impossible to get through the surf — waiting with anxiety for a lull to get on board, I was taken prisoner, forwarded to Hobart Gaol, committed for trial *for being illegally at large under a Second Conviction* sentenced *death*.

The humane Captain Welsh again interceded for me &
saved my life though I was not acquainted with it until morning
-— I was pinioned and going out to be executed. I was then
conveyed on board the Brig *Prince Leopold* for Macquarie Harbour
— I arrived there after 16 days dreadful weather. I was landed
and taken before the Commandant, being the only prisoner sent
down in the brig — I found him every thing but a gentleman — a
complete Tyrant. He ordered what clothes I had on to be burned
and gave me a suit of yellow and sent to work, and at night to be
sent to an Island where there was upward of 200 of what he called
out and outers — men who would strain every point to get away.

It was a most wretched place for the most common
necessaries of comfort — hours before day we were roused and a
pint of miserable thin gruel was allowed each man — *Into the boats*
was the word, and then we had to remain in a bleak wind and all
weathers till daylight when we were mustered, lead to our work

31

and getting nothing to eat until we again returned to the Island which would be very likely dark, wet through and not a spark of fire to dry our clothes before we were again drove out. Nothing but misery, flogging and starvation — murders were frequently committed — twice or three times a month — with a view of ridding themselves of a wretched existence. Out of every 100 young men 96 would have sore backs, in fact so bad was the treatment that death was preferable.

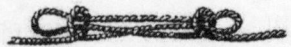

I was labouring under this dreadful state of things for 12 months and upwards until at last I got a slight chance for liberty — so strong was this feeling that I was fully determined to gain my point or perish in the attempt. The case was this: 20 of us were going over on the main to Kelly's Bason to get some logs on the pits for sawyers. We made it up to rush the launch, take her by force, and take over land for it — tho' we had two great risks to run, one of being starved to death as many had been, the other of being killed by the blacks as they were very numerous about the S.W. Cape. The moment we reached Kelly's Bason, myself and two more, Sheedy & William Holt, took all the tools out of the launch to deprive any person who may have felt inclined to resist us. We then ordered every man to remain in the launch, and those men that were first to propose it sat down in the bottom of the launch and never stirred. We found it was left to the three of us, so we made the best use of our time, the three of us jumped into the launch armed with tomahawks. My two companions stood over them while I threw the oars overboard to prevent them from getting back to the Settlement to give an alarm — and to give us an opportunity to get over the Sugar Loaf Mountain.

We took from them whatever we required, got out of the launch and shoved them clear of the landing place. We then started for the Mountain and no sooner had we gained the summit than we could see a boat coming to the assistance of the launch. We then made for Phillip Island Creek to get there by night to plunder them, when all was quiet, of provisions to carry us across the Mountains. We succeeded without interruption & went from hut to hut and secured them as we plundered them — we served 32 men in this manner and got a good deal of provisions. We concealed our plunder and the same night swam to Phillip Island, made the three men there get out of their beds and shew us where their canoe was. They did so — for it was concealed as it was prohibited (they had it for fishing). We took her ashore where our provisions was and concealed her among the long grass at the edge of the water until next night, daylight being so near at hand & all being correct.

We discovered a Whale Boat, a Gig & Launch making for the Station where we were. They landed, and the Commandant being there ordered the whole of the Gang into the launch and they all returned to the Settlement, leaving five of the military and giving them orders to shoot us if they could *come near us* — we could hear the whole of these orders. As soon as night came we got into the Canoe and pulled for the Gordon's River where if we reached the source of it we would soon reach Headquarters — *Hobart Town* — and gave a better chance of our liberty. It was daybreak when we reached the entrance of the river and we could see the Settlement from where we then were. We passed unobserved and that night reached Guy Fawke's Creek and being very much fatigued we camped for the night without being disturbed. The next morning we got on our legs again and in sweeping a deep bay to keep clear of the current we kept close to the shore, when a launch with a gang of men going to fell pine showed around the point pulling as hard as they could after us — they got the weather gage of us and rushed us fairly in shore. We had to take to the mountains without a bit of food, being closely pursued, and we would rather famish than go back.

The launch returned to the Settlement taking the canoe with them — leaving us in a most wretched condition, nothing on but our shirts, trowsers — & nothing but small fern around us from the inclemency of the weather. We lay down in the wet, laying close to each other for warmth, & what with despair and misery we fell into a sleep (as it were of death) and knew nothing until we were roused by the firing of musketry over our heads by the

Military. We could not walk, they had to get us to the Boat by carrying us — in this wretched state we were brought back to the Settlement and in this state we were ordered by the Commandant to a dark cell in the Gaol, and I certainly think I would have died had it not been for a Sergeant's Wife who brought us nourishment two or three times in the course of the night — the Doctor was equally as bad as the Commandant.

In the morning to our great satisfaction we heard the vessel had arrived with another Commandant — we had scarce time to rejoice when we were taken to the office and sentenced 300 lashes — *100 every Monday for 3 successive weeks* — this being Saturday we were tried on. We were being flogged when Major Bailey came ashore but was fairly disgusted with our treatment, seeing our wretched appearance, and enquired into our case, which the Tyrant finding out, altered our days of punishment and we received our 200 lashes the next day more dead than alive. This so much enraged Major Bailey when we explained our case to him that he took charge sooner than he otherwise would have done and took the power out of his hands — no more sad countenances, when Major Bailey took charge — all was joy beaming in every countenance. The Brig sailed for Hobart Town — and left tranquillity on the Island.

A Whale Boat in crossing the Bar was capsized & all hands with the Pilot were drowned — I was sent down by the Major to take charge of a Boat. At this time a *Brig* called the *Frederic* was on the Stocks, and they were getting very forward with her when orders were sent down by the Governor Arthur that all prisoners were to be removed to *Port Arthur* — I was with others determined if possible to remain behind and once more chance our lives for our liberty. A Captain was down acting as Pilot and was also to take the Brig to Hobart Town when fitted out. I was at this time the Coxswain to the Pilot Boat & wishing the Brig was ready.

Knowing for certain that Macquarie Harbour was to be abolished and not being certain to remain to go up in the *Frederic* when finished, I contrived a plan to obtain my liberty thus: the Commandant had a small boat called the *Saint Patrick*. I rigged her as a cutter for him & I generally went with him in rough weather — I came to a determination to capsize her and swim with the Major ashore. Should I succeed I should be sure of a pardon of my Colonial sentence: I had tried all the schemes to obtain my liberty in a manly manner, and this was the only one I could pick upon to save me from going to Port Arthur, another wretched Penal Settlement.

The time came, I chaffed the lanyards of the water breakers which we used for ballast, so that when the boat made a surge they would break and fall to leeward and assist in capsizing us. As soon as we neared Badger Rock I knew we would get a smart puff of wind which I was in hopes would answer my purpose — she caught it before the beam which hove her down on her broadside. I made the stay foresail & jib sheets fast — away went the breakers to leeward. I also fell as an accident, but all would not do — she turned out stiff as a crutch — she righted — the Major eased off the main sheet — jib sheet to windward hove her round on her heel, and we returned home — he being quite satisfied at not going overboard.

A few days after this I was sent for by the Major where there was company at his house, consisting of A.C.General Woldrobe & Lady, Ensign Bishop & Sister & Captain Harris of the Brig *Derwent*. After I had staged a few sea-songs the Major asked me if I could swim or not — I replied I could, well. He asked me, would I have saved him supposing the boat capsized when we were taken in the squall. I told him yes. He said it was his opinion (since) that I wished the boat to upset on that day & that he would now give me a good dram of grog if I would tell him in the presence of the Company. I told him I would tell the truth without any liquor — and I gave him the real truth with my motive for so doing — caused a smile amongst the Company. The Major pitied me and forgave, as he said, my *experiment* at the hazard of his life but also remarked that had I succeeded my pardon was sure — I thanked the good Major & returned to my Hut. It appeared to me that after so many attempts I was certainly born under an unlucky star.

In the month of November 1833 two vessels came to Macquarie Harbour to convey all the prisoners (to Port Arthur & Hobart Town) with the exception of ten that were to be left to finish the Brig out and to return with her to Hobart Town — I was one of the ten picked out by the Major and I was very pleased at the news. All hands were busy that were going to Port Arthur packing up their things, all was noise and confusion, and in a fortnight all the prisoners were on board that were going to Head Quarters. Our good Commandant (Major Bailey) was also going to leave us. I felt as much parting with him as from a parent, & I cannot help saying *God prosper him wherever he is!* Before going he gave strict orders to the Pilot who was going to have charge of the Brig to put the whole of us (i.e. the ten prisoners) on Marine Rations and a gill of rum per diem, & that when he got to Head Quarters he would intercede for a ticket of leave for the whole of us, if we behaved ourselves on the way to Hobart Town. We thanked him and bid farewell to our kind Commandant with three cheers. They got under weigh and were soon out of sight.

We commenced our work with a good heart. These are the names of the men left for the fitting out of the Brig: James Porter, William Shires, John Barker (our navigator) John Fare (formerly Captain of the Forecastle of the *Genoa74*) James Leslie, Benjamin Russen, John Riley and the two monsters Cheshire & Lyons (of whom I shall have much to speak about in the sequel). There were only nine of us determined to take the Brig — Cheshire (the Traitor) did not know of it at first but merely found it out by accident: the hut he was in was only divided by a partition where

Leslie & Russen were conversing about the Brig when Cheshire heard the whole of the plot and informed Barker — Cheshire was at this time cooking for him. Barker informed the rest of us. We did not know what to do, knowing he had proved a perjured Villain on two or three occasions while on the Island. We at last came to the conclusion to tell him he should go and to keep all a secret — he assured us he would.

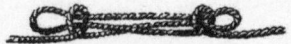

All went on well. On the 12th January 1834 we took our departure from the Island of Misery. That evening we made the Heads where we let go our anchor. Two of us, Cheshire and myself, were ordered by the Captain Taw to pull the boat ashore and bring off some potatoes. Mr. Hoy, a Master Ship Builder, and two soldiers went on shore with us, but previous to our going we told our companions that if they got a *slant o' wind* (a chance) to take her while we were on shore — to hoist the Ensign Union downwards & we would disarm those who were on shore, come on board and leave them behind. This they agreed to but did not get an opportunity. The moment we got on board, the wind setting in from N.W. dead on shore, a heavy swell set in and we were forced to turn back to a place called Wellington Head and there come to anchor. This was on the 12th at night, all passed on well, and in the morning we asked to go on shore to wash our clothes with a view to having our Pistols ready, for we expected a bit of a round turn with them, there being nine of them and ten of us.

The names of the party in the Brig were Captain Taw, Mr. Hoy (Ship Builder) William Nichols, steward, McFarlane, a free man, James Tait, mate, and four soldiers who slept on the aft deck. The Pistols and Tomahawk we had were made by John Barker — pistols made from old Musket Barrels — as he was Overseer of Smiths and a most ingenious man at anything. We returned on board as soon as possible and went down into the forecastle, we did not wish to shed blood.

I hit on a plan to get rid of two soldiers & McFarlane by persuading the Sergeant to go and ask the Whale Boat to go fishing. The Captain granted it — I *gammoned* that the Cramp had taken me in the stomach and according went without me, which left three short of their number which made a great odds in our favour. I asked the other two soldiers to come down to the forecastle to hear some singing. One of them came, the other sat on the windlass and Russen & Leslie & Cheshire were on deck, the other seven of us were in the forecastle with one soldier. I began to Sing *"The Grand Conversation Lies under the Rose"*, but I could not get on, my mind was in such a state — Shires helped me out with it.

The signal was given on deck by stamping from Russen — when Shires put a pistol to the head of the soldier, who was quiet directly — me & Shires rushed on deck, I put the Hatch on the fore scuttle dragging a small kedge anchor to put on it for security, when Leslie came with the other soldier and Shires with the Mate.

40

I lifted off the Hatch and let the rest of our companions on deck and ordered the Mate and the soldier to go below, putting the Hatch on and leaving them in the charge of Riley. We then crept slowly aft (all the foregoing was done without any noise) and sneaked down the aft deck, got the whole of the Muskets & Ball Cartridge belonging to them. The Captain, Carpenter and Steward were drinking in the Cabin (our rum, for they did not give us what was ordered, after the Commandant left).

When we had the arms secured we heard a Bustle in the Cabin, pulled the skylight off, when we seen Shires struggling with three of them, the whole of them endeavouring to take his life (they being nearly drunk). However he succeeded in getting on deck before we could render him any assistance — I removed the compass to a place of safety. We then spoke to them in the Cabin to come on deck and we would not injure them. But they being groggy, they refused to do so, defying the whole of us — now and then presenting their Pistols and Muskets at us. They kept us at bay for a long time for we did not wish to injure them, though they were in our power if we had thought proper to have fired upon them, and we knew to rush upon drunken men some lives must be lost.

At length, being tired of persuading them to surrender we were determined to frighten them. Then the word was *Fire down upon them!* (with no intention of so doing), when letting fall our muskets upon the comings of the Hatch with too much violence, the sudden jar caused one of them to go off and a Ball knocked a bunch of keys out of the Captain's hands as he was going to unlock an arms chest; this had the desired effect and they cried out for quarters.

We ordered them on deck one by one when we lashed their hands behind them and fired off a musket as a signal for the Whale Boat to come alongside — they answered the signal and very soon made their appearance alongside. The moment they did I jumped into the main chains and ordered them to make fast the Whale Boat painter and get into the Brig's Jolly Boat that was hanging alongside. They did so, a man was placed as Sentinel over them to prevent them coming on board. This being done, myself, John Barker and Shires went down to the Cabin with Captain Taw and Mr Hoy, as they requested us to give them some clothing. We allowed them to take anything they wanted — they wanted a pistol and some ammunition from us to protect them from the blacks (as they wished to make us believe), but we *begged to be excused!!* Having got what they wanted we ordered them upon the deck one by one. We fastened Captain Taw's hands owing to his complaining of a bad back, we then ordered the Mate and the two soldiers up from the forecastle and bid them go over the side into the Jolly Boat. We then ordered the Steward over & assisted Mr. Hoy over, loosened the Captain's hands and passed him over the side. The whole of them were then in the Jolly Boat, we then ordered them to shove off from the Brig and lay on their oars. Six of us then manned the Whale Boat (armed), two of us pulling & four on guard: we guarded them to the shore, when we ordered them to get out of the boat and shove her into deep water towards us, to prevent them from rushing upon our boat.

We returned to the Brig and got some refreshment for we had tasted nothing that day, so great was our anxiety to get the Brig. It was now dark (we selected one George Williams as cook, I forgot to mention his name before). We then divided the remaining nine of us into three watches for the night, and to sing out *All's Well* every half hour — for we had two Good Watches belonging to the Captain & Mr. Hoy. We kept a strict watch that night and in the morning at daybreak we hoisted all the provisions on deck, and there being nine of them on shore and ten of us on board, we equally divided the provisions & put one half on shore for them & the other half we put down in the aft deck.

We armed ourselves & went on shore, it being very early. We hailed them where they were encamped, Captain Taw was coming to us but we ordered him back and inquired for Mr. Hoy. He came & brought two soldiers with him. We ordered the soldiers to come into the water to the boat for their provisions & we soon emptied the boat — we asked Mr. Hoy if there was anything else we could oblige him with — he wished for some strengthening plaster and bandages from his chest for a pain in the back — the soldiers also wished for their watch coats. We returned to the Brig & brought all they desired — we also brought the only two bottles of wine on board to Mr. Hoy, being unwell. (*This was proved on our trial.*) Mr. Hoy asked us if we would give up the Brig & he would swear on a Bible never to say a word about the matter. We declined any such thing. He said:

Since I find you will not deliver her up — I thank you for your manly conduct throughout, and particularly for your kindness to me on

43

account of my illness. I know you have but little provisions to cross the wide ocean, and likewise a vessel that is not Seaworthy for such a voyage – and may God prosper you in your perilous undertaking.

We thanked him and pulled off our hats amid the loud cheers of all on shore wishing us a *Pleasant Voyage*. I cannot express my feelings at that moment – my heart expanded within me, and I believe it was the happiest moment of my life. We observed Mr. Hoy wiping his eyes. We felt for him and that was all we *could* do in our situation.

We came alongside the Brig, got on board – clapt to and hove the anchor short – others were employed in letting go the kedge anchor ahead to commence her out. In the meantime I went on shore taking an axe with me and broke up a 6-oared gig in case any accident happened to the Brig they could not surprise us – I then hastened on board and commenced the laborious task of warping her out three miles to the sea gate. We were compelled to do this as we wished to start soon, as we expected another vessel from Hobart Town in search of the *Frederic* as she was then over her time. We succeeded in getting her abreast of two islands called the *Cap and Bonnet* – the boat we hung astern, and in another hour the tide was running at the rate of 7 knots an hour in our favour – we got the Whale Boat manned, sent her ahead to check her now and then when she yawed. We got through the sea gate, the current being so strong our helm & the boat ahead was no use to us, she heeled round in spite of us — we were fearful of her striking on the North Spit — a light air of wind now favoured us, we loosened our sails, got steerage way on her. We edged her off clear of all danger — the moment we got outside of the reefs the breeze freshened from W.N.W. We found we should have no use for the Whale Boat, we broke her up, took the oars with us. This was on the 14th January 1834 when we took our final farewell of Macquarie Harbour Heads with light hearts.

It was then that John Barker commenced his duty as Navigator, (which he learned at the Settlement from a prisoner named William Harry Phillips, once in the East India Company Service). We divided ourselves into two watches, there being only four seamen on board, the other six were landsmen, which caused the duty to fall heavy on us four. We also found Mr. Hoy's remark too true — for no sooner had we got into sea way with the Brig than she leaked to an alarming degree. We got the pumps to work and they were kept going all the voyage — we dare not neglect them two hours at a time — the breeze freshened to a heavy gale by the next morning the 15th at 8 o'clock from N.W. — we were running 12 knots under a single reefed main top sail & fore sail in a heavy sea & for nine days and nights she required two of us at the helm.

Van Diemens Land

On the 24th the gale broke and we carried a stiff top gallant quarterly breeze for four weeks with a heavy range of sea after us. A villain named Lyon let the main boom jibe on him & carried it away — McFare and myself fished it & made it firm as ever, but during the time we had this quarterly wind — after three weeks running our navigator found we were going too far southward & brought her nearer the wind. This gave the sea greater power on the Brig and alarmed Lyons that was at the helm, & coward-like persuaded the watch to square the yards & run the vessel before it for the whole watch (four hours), which made scores of miles difference to us — and also, endeavouring to deceive us he brought the Brig upon the wind again, but at 12 o'clock the next day when Barker took the Sun he found out the mistake. When the rascals were taxed with this gross neglect of duty they told the truth, & we were going to give Lyons a short passage over the side — but all ended in peace and it was looked over with a caution not to do the like again at his peril or he should certainly *die*.

We still continued on our way with prosperous gales — we found our provisions getting very scant & obliged to issue a certain small portion every day. The only vessel we fell in with was a French Whaler running along the coast — the moment we seen her we got our arms and ammunition upon deck, for had she hoisted her Ensign we could not have answered her not having a flag or bit of bunting on board, and had they come alongside and made themselves inquisitive we were determined to run on board of them, capture them, or die in the attempt. For we knew if we were brought back Governor Arthur would *hang* us to a *dead* certainty. They however passed us, and in a few days after we sighted the main land of South America on the 27th February — after six weeks & one day of a passage, and proud we were of it as the Brig was getting the best of us in the leakage. We immediately got to work with the little strength we had remaining, got a purchase on the main & fore yard to hoist out our long boat of 7 tons — Shires, Leslie and Russen put another streak on her and decked her in case we should have to quit the Brig.

During the time the Brig was thus laying to I questioned the whole of my companions what story we should have when we reached the shore as there was no doubt of us being overhauled by them when we landed — we made up a plausible yarn — but when I came to cross-question them I found they were all upon their guard with the exception of Cheshire, who being quite indifferent as to what he should say, I told the rest of my companions it was my opinion that if they *pinched* him (Cheshire) he would *come-it* (tell the *whole* truth) and hang the whole of us. They were all of my opinion as we knew him to be a determined villain previous to his coming to us. I made no hesitation in snatching a pistol, cocked it, & said that I should save *our* lives at the expense of his. I was up on the last step of the companion ladder with this full determination *settling* him, when Barker prevented me, desiring me not to shed blood, & he should be put on shore the first land we made to. I was vexed & threw the pistol on the cabin floor with such violence that it went off — I said I could put up with hanging as well as any of them!

Van Diemens Land

We got the long boat out with great difficulty and put what little things we had into her. As for provisions we had not more than 2 lbs (bread and meat) — we dropped the long boat astern & sloop rigged her. We had neglected pumping the vessel ever since we sighted land being employed at other things. We found the sooner we got out of her the better, and it was not until dark that night we could leave her, being fairly knocked up with over exertion and little to eat. However we took our leave of her, hove her to as she was approaching the shore which we calculated about 40 miles off — and I never left my parents with more regret nor was my feelings harrowed up to such a pitch as when I took a last farewell of the smart little *Frederic*.

The Brig stood to Seaward, and in the state she was in, water logged & so much dead weight for ballast — she soon went down. All things being ready, up sail and ran in for land, & when we thought we had run long enough we hauled our wind & stretched along the land. When daylight appeared we could see the shore close aboard of us covered with a rich verdure.

End Part Two

PART THREE

Chile

1834-36

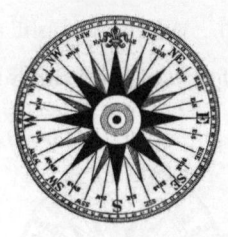

Golden Cap
Figure in Chilean Landscape
Conrad Martens
Dixon Library, State Library of NSW

PART THREE

Chile

1834−1836

We ran along the coast the best part of that day when we observed a large bay − getting our oars out we pulled her into it, found a lee for our boat and all of us went ashore & got a great many shellfish which was to us a great luxury; we also brought our Tom Cat with us from the Brig − it left us and was away all night and returned early next morning, but shortly left us entirely. At 12 o'clock, this being the second day since we left the Brig, we killed a seal, & not finding the Cat we left some of the flesh ashore for it and took our departure from the Bay. In three months after we were landed we found out the very place where the cat was endeavouring to call our attention to was where the Rio Beuon emptied itself & had we followed the Cat he would have conducted us to the Indian inhabitants and saved us a deal of trouble.

We proceeded along the coast the remainder of that day, and coming on night a smart breeze sprung up, when we had great doubts concerning our little boat weathering the night. Providence befriended us in this manner for six days, when on the sixth night we weathered Tweedale Point, so named in the chart, which projects a long way out to sea, and in about half an hour after we got round it we heard a noise on shore like a Bullock or Cow. We looked earnestly and to our surprise we saw a fire. We made towards it and soon perceived some human beings about it. We hailed them when they, being surprised, gave a kind of yell.

However we tried what water we had, we found it too deep for us so we neared the shore a little more and brought up in 22 fathoms. We remained there until morning and pulled in shore towards some kelp or seaweed, making a line fast to it. We then steered her in towards the rocks where the Indians were, each with a knife in his belt — we had our belts on and each man with a brace of Pistols in them. The moment the boat was nigh enough to jump out, five of us got on shore, the other five hauling the boat off to the sea weed she was made fast to. Acting with this precaution we considered if we met with a hostile reception it was far better for five of us to lose our lives than ten of us.

This movement of ours astonished the natives. They brought us to their dwellings which was very clean & neat. I also perceived they understood agriculture, which gave us good hopes of gaining information. I enquired for provisions, shewing them some gold, but I found they could not or would not understand me. I then enquired for Valdivia. They understood me perfectly well and informed me it was three leagues off, being nine miles. I returned to the boat overjoyed and told my companions the news which pleased them much. We gave them a few trinkets, which pleased them much, and took our departure, and the same afternoon we reached the desired port of Valdivia & landed safe, hungry enough.

When we were within 100 yards of the landing place off the fort several of the inhabitants came down to meet us, and pointed to us where to bring our boat in with safety. We went in at high water and when the tide ebbed the boat was left high and dry. Five of our number were conducted by the natives to their dwellings and remained four hours amongst them (they taking us for Seamen, shipwrecked) and then returned to our boat and the other five went amongst the inhabitants. We found them a very humane race of people — yet some of the lower class shewed a great disposition for thieving which made us keep a strict watch on them.

The whole of us remained with the boat that night and the next morning we came to a conclusion that the tradesmen should go to the town which was nine miles up the river as though they had come from Chiloa, being given to understand that there was a vessel there on the stocks and plenty of work to be had. They immediately hired a canoe for nine dollars which they cheerfully gave — we bid them farewell for we never expected to see them more, as we intended to launch our boat the next day and get under way for Valparaiso where I knew if my wife, children and friends were alive I should remain during my life and return thanks to God that I did not founder on the rocks of despair.

We endeavoured to launch the boat but we found our endeavours in vain owing to her being high and dry. We were therefore compelled to let her remain till the next day in hopes of getting sufficient water under her to float her off. The remainder of that day & night we enjoyed ourselves very much with the Patriots, dancing & singing to the guitar — the next morning we slept over late and were roused up by the Military & an Officer sent down by the Intendant or Governor to conduct us to the town where our companions was confined. They seized our long boat and launched her into the water, manning her with some of the soldiers, and late that evening we arrived in the town and were confined apart from the other five of our companions in a place called the Quartell.

Several of the Officers visited us when we asked the reason we were confined, but they gave us no Satisfaction. In the course of that night a Sergeant named Jago Orutea came to us & brought us some Aquadent — I offered him a dollar but he refused it until I pressed upon him very much. I then questioned him if he knew why we were detained, and having a faint knowledge of the Castilian we could understand each other. He informed me that one of the first five who came in the Canoe had been drinking with a man called Cockney Tom, and that he believed he had been saying *too* much to him about our circumstances & that was the cause of *our* confinement. I told him to wait a few minutes, I wrote a note with pencil — put it in a bit of bread & sent the bread to Barker — I stated that my Suspicions fell on Cheshire — I soon got an answer by Jago (in the same manner as I sent). Barker thought it was only their suspicions & could not believe anyone could be so mad — however I was uneasy.

We remained in confinement a week when the very crew of the French Whaler that crossed our stern a few days before at sea were brought in as prisoners — it appears they were wrecked — but the Captain showed his papers & they were immediately released. The Governor too had gone on a party of pleasure to the Imperial, a place where some civilized Indians resided. In the course of a fortnight he returned — and a fine, noble looking fellow he was. The day after he arrived we were all ordered to the Palaza to be examined — we were ushered in to a spacious & elegant apartment, a large table in the centre, the Governor sat at one end & a great number of Officers were present — an interpreter was then introduced — a Captain Lawson (a smuggler) — he commanded a Schooner on the coast and a regular terror he was to them.

We were asked where did we sail from — where & when first sprung a leak, where was our Captain & papers, etc. etc. I was selected to answer the questions — I answered them all as I thought satisfactorily — the Brig's glass and Brass sheaves of the blocks we had with us in the boat were then brought forward — I accounted for them by stating that the British Government often have a sale of old stores & all things were sold with the Government *mark* in them — and that the owners in the Merchant Service would not trouble themselves in taking them out. Still there was something doubtful in the mind of the Governor — he said *Call Thomas,* when the redoubtable Cockney Tom made his appearance — he was asked by the Governor if all he had stated privately to him was a fact. He said *Yes* and retired — which quite astonished us.

The Governor was silent for a few minutes then said:

Sailors, you have come on this Coast in a clandestine manner and though you put a good face on your story I have every reason to believe you are Pirates, and unless you state the truth between this and tomorrow at 8 o'clock, I shall give orders for you all to be shot — take them away!

Avast there, said I, *a word with you upon the subject. We as sailors shipwrecked and in distress expected when we made this port to have been treated in a Christianlike manner, not as though we were dogs! Is this the way you would have treated us when the British Tars were fighting for your independence and bleeding in your cause against the old Spaniards? And if we were Pirates do you suppose we should be so weak as to cringe to your Tyranny? Never! I also wish you to understand that if we are shot, England will know of it and will be revenged — you will find us in the same mind tomorrow as we are in now, and should you put*

56

your threat into execution, tomorrow we shall teach you Patriots how to die!

All was quiet for a minute or two — a Lieutenant Day was sent for. He was asked if he had any knowledge of me when he was with Lord Cochrane. He said I was only a boy when on board with him, but though a long time ago yet he had some knowledge of me and in particular my voice. When I was asked some questions concerning the Fort at Corrall they seemed satisfied, but orders were given to return us to the Quartell. This was about 12 o'clock and we were still kept apart; about half past 1 o'clock news came to us that Cheshire had been absent nearly half an hour and they did not know where he was, but we soon heard for a fact that he had stated the whole facts of the case fearful of what would follow. I stated to my companions that there was only one way to baffle Cheshire's expectations, that if we still denied being the men after such convincing proofs we should be in the manner of giving him sufficient room to hang us and escape himself. Therefore I proposed that if we went before the Governor next day we should state the whole truth to him — to do away with Cheshire's evidence and include him in the number. This was willingly agreed to by the rest, and accordingly the next day we were ushered before the Governor.

He asked us if we still persisted against the approver — I told him the whole of our circumstances but also stated that we would rather have died than stated anything of our affair, but our motive in doing so was that Cheshire should not escape but share the same fate as us, and as we had stated the facts of the case we hoped he, the Governor, would not put Cheshire's name down in his despatches as the approver. He said he would do as we wished and that he should fare as the rest — we all thanked him. The Governor then turned to Cheshire and said:

Had you been a South American instead of what you are, all the forces I command could not have stopped the rabble from tearing you to pieces!

He then spoke to us telling us he did not wish to keep us confined and if we would pass our words that we would not endeavour to make our escape he would allow us to go about on Parole of Honour (!!) as there was plenty of work for the whole of us, and that he would get a petition signed by himself and the principal inhabitants and forward it to the Supreme Government at Santiago informing him that we had thrown ourselves on their protection — and he had no doubt of a favourable answer — he then discharged us.

Cheshire asked the Governor to protect him, that he knew if James Porter came across him he would take his life — we were called back, who said:

This man Cheshire is afraid of his life, therefore I am duty bound to protect him as well as the rest of you. Therefore, as he is a bit of a carpenter he shall reside near me, and when he wants to go abroad one of my orderlies shall go with him, and I hope you in particular Porter will not molest him.

I made no answer. We went to the Quartell and brought what things belonged to us, and there were plenty of the inhabitants ready to receive us with open arms.

I fell in with a kind friend named Don Lopez, a merchant, had a wife and four children who were soon very fond of me — two days after our release the Governor requested us to attend a Ship Launch, which had been three years on the stocks, which we did, and she went off in a masterly manner. He also employed us at fitting her out at 16$ per month (4 weeks). After this I returned to my friend Lopez who would not allow me to work for any person, but remain with him and consider myself as one of the family.

I thanked him — it was all I could do at that time. However in the course of a few days Don Lopez informed me he had a great quantity of valuable skins about fifty miles up the river, but the whirlpools or rapids were so strong that the boat became unmanageable, the cargo generally lost and also lives at the same time. I told him if he would get me a small boat and crew I would go up the river and have a look at it and then I should be able to judge the better. I went and came back and informed him that I would venture to take a launch up, and if the Peons (oarsmen) would do as I told them there would be no fear. He was glad to hear this and said he would accompany me, which caused a great many *Ave Marias* to escape the lips of his wife for our safety.

All things being ready we got underweigh with a larger launch pulling 16 oars double bank. As soon as we came to the Rio Primero, which was 25 miles, the men got some refreshment & started again — we reached there all safe, got the cargo aboard & prepared to return. I found a rudder was no use. I immediately unshipped it, got a long oar to steer with & a strong Indian alongside of me in case I should require him when I got near the whirlpools. We reached home in safety, which was the first time of a cargo coming safe.

All went well but the despatches had not arrived at this time. There was a lady of Don Lopez's acquaintance called Donna Inez Ascension who begged, as a favour from Lopez, to use his interest in her behalf in persuading me to go and live at her place during the time the slaves were making Cyder, to protect her and her little son & property — the question was asked me if I would go — I felt for her and consented, not knowing the spitfire I should have to deal with. I took leave of my friends & they parted with me as if I was their own child, and begged of me to return as soon as Cyder was completed. I said I should — and it was not until dark at night we reached the Segunda Cruz, a half-mile from her house. This we had to go by water — it being up the river and late.

I knew very little about the place, however next morning her son came to me and informed me my breakfast was ready. She called Antoinette, a handsome slave girl about 16 years of age to clean the breakfast things away — she informed me she gave a cow and a hatchet for her to an Indian Cacique. She then came outside, called all the 23 slaves and gave them to understand I was their Master. They went to work: everything was in my charge.

At 12 o'clock that day she went visiting. It was then that I heard this lady's character from Antoinette, which caused me to wish to leave, when she came home. However, I was put upon my guard, and I had been there about three months when she thought I was too kind to Antoinette, and for which reason she tied her up by the thumbs to a crop piece in the barn with her toes scarcely touching the ground. Young Diego, her son, informed me of this. I immediately went and cut her down, which so enraged her mistress that she immediately bound her up again. I again took her down — and the lady ran to a drawer & rushed at me with a carving knife — I tript her up and took the knife out of her hands. She got up, ran into the room and brought another with a determination to take my life. I felt enraged at this and I was standing behind [a chair] & as she made a plunge at me I lifted the chair of a sudden and struck her on the head, leaving her, as I supposed, dead on the ground.

I felt rather sorry for striking her but when I seen the knife alongside of her I went directly, got my bag and clothes with an intention to leave. I also went to Antoinette & persuaded her to go with me & I would find her a better master which was Don Lopez. She consented and off we went, leaving the boy Diego crying — for us leaving. I went to an Alcalde and informed him of what had happened, when he said it was what she deserved, for her cruel disposition was the cause of her husband's shooting himself. I wished to get a Canoe to take me and the Indian girl down the river, he informed me I could not get one until the morning — I could remain in his house till then.

I thanked him, but in the course of that day the lady came to herself & found out where I was & sent some neighbours to me. I went back to her & she was a sad spectacle for the Comb had stuck in her head. However by over persuasion I returned, with Antoinette, & all was well again in a month, and Lady Ascension proved altered for the better and gained the good will of all her neighbours. It went on well for about two months when I was noticed by getting three large guns up on their carriages for the Military, who came to protect our village from the threatened invasion of the Indians.

Another incident happened to me shortly after this which nearly cost me my life. The Military often came to the house of the Lady Ascension during the time of the Cider, and one afternoon my mistress was taking a Siesta when a black Sergeant, a Corporal and two privates came for the express purpose (being nearly drunk) of plundering the place of the Cider & aquadent. When the boy Diego came and informed me of it I then ran out and seen them forcing the door. I rushed upon the nearest and knocked him down with my fist, the other three seeing this drew their sabres and advanced towards me — the boy Diego came up and put a long hunting spear into my hand — I advanced to drive them off the premises when they divided themselves to surround me. I darted at the Sergeant and wounded him in the breast, he fell, the Corporal made a cut at me but missed me. I turned at him, when the three retreated. I then went to the Sergeant who was bleeding and brought him into the house, bound his wounds; he begged of me not to mention it to the Officers. I gave him my word and he left me satisfied and went to the fort.

Not so the other three. They found a Peon, made him half drunk & gave him some money to kill me with his sealing knife. I took a walk this evening towards the Magistrate's house — there was a number of men drinking Cider — when I came opposite to this miscreant with his knife under his Poncho or Mantle, he asked me for a loan of my pipe — I did not like to refuse him — I gave it to him and waited a long time to see if he would return it. I asked him for it — he threw my pipe on the ground which broke it, thinking I would stoop to pick it up and then he would have stabbed me. But seeing my pipe broke, my passion arose in a moment and I struck him in the face — the calves of his legs came in contact with a trough they used for making Cider in — it

63

capsized him, and in trying to save himself he exposed the open knife. I flew at him and took it forcibly away from him while his companions were gazing at me.

Margeretta the Magistrate's daughter saw the whole of the transaction and begged of me to come into the house, but I was so much vexed at the treatment that I went home, determined to quit that place where there was so much villainy. On my return home I met Lieutenant Martell in company with the Lady Ascension. He nodded to me but me being in a passion did not return it, and I threw myself upon the strow (a sofa) to give vent to my feelings. When Lieutenant Martell came to me he asked me what was the cause of my passing him in such a sulky mood. I answered him I had great cause for being so, nor did I wish to state my grievance to him (knowing his fiery temper I did not wish to cause any disturbance) but on the morrow I should take my departure for Valdivia. The Officer then left me apparently in a passion. I went to the Box for my wearing apparel and was in the act of securing them for my departure in the morning, when Lieutenant Martell came to me with a hasty step (Patriot-like) in a great rage and said he was informed by the Magistrate's daughter who was a witness to the whole proceedings, and furthermore, the man that wanted to take my life was now confined on a small island in the centre of the river, by his orders, and he would use his exertions to have him shot the next day, and before I could give him an answer he had quitted my sight. I now began to study what was to be done, to save the culprit's life, when I was aroused from my reverie by a young woman with an infant in her arms, who thus accosted me:

Don Santiago O'Connor, (my name being at that time James O'Connor) *I have been given to understand my husband is to be shot tomorrow for attempting your life, when elevated with liquor.*

Her sobbing choked her utterance when she presented me the baby. I took the child from her and kissed it, when she asked me, almost stifled in tears, whether I would save the child's father by forgiving him, or leave him to perish, herself would then be a widow and the child fatherless in the wide world. My heart ached for her in her present situation, and I told her frankly to make herself easy on that point, that save him I would, in hope that he never would commit a treacherous act of the same kind again. She would have fallen on her knees but I sternly prevented her. She took the child from me, made a curtsy, but apparently her heart was too full of gratitude to make any further reply. She then left the room.

I felt somewhat relieved after this interview and was happy to think it was in my power to save a miserable being from an ignominious Death and also to be the means of making them happy once again. That day and night passed, when early in the morning Sergeant Orutea came for me by order of the Captain. I made my appearance at the fort and was ushered into an apartment where sat the Captain, the two Lieutenants, the Magistrate and a few of the respectable inhabitants, and in about five minutes the culprit made his appearance, with only a pair of trousers on and shirt, shivering with the cold. He appeared to be very much alarmed. The Captain informed him of his proceedings and asked him what he thought of himself. He said he was in liquor and knew nothing of the transaction. This would not clear him, I plainly could see what would follow if I did not put an end to it, so I thus began.

Gentlemen, it is true I am an Englishman, the only one among you, yet I look with the same degree of pleasure on all around me as though it were my native soil. Gratitude for the Kindness and Protection I have received since my arrival on this land, from the Cavaliers residing in the Province of Valdivia, compels me thus to express my feelings: that I consider myself thus far a true Patriot, that I am ready at any moment when required to fight, and rather than flinch, expire under the Patriot Flag!

All eyes were upon me but not a word spoke. I took an advantage of their silence and asked them to grant me one request. They said they could not deny me.

Then, as I freely forgive yon mad-brained fellow, striving to take my life when in a state of intoxication, I hope, Gentlemen, that you will coincide with my feelings and acquit him for this time, for the sake of his wife and infant.

They all appeared to be amazed when at last the Captain spoke:

Here is a contrast of great magnitude (directing his discourse to the trembling sealer) *it was only yesterday you were contriving to take this generous Englishman's life, and now he is supplicating to save yours! For shame of you! And from this moment never, never forget the villainy on your side and the compassion of this foreigner on the other. Go, quit my sight, and ever bear in mind it is to this generous sailor you are indebted to your life.*

It took great impression on the prisoner, and with eyes full of tears he bowed, gave a glance at me that I shall never forget, and then went out to his wife who was happy to receive him. He had scarcely got away when the two privates, the Corporal, and Sergeant, that I had prevented from robbing the premises, came in and thus addressed the Officers.

We are the men who bribed the sealer to take the sailor's life (for reasons best known to ourselves) but after having heard him plead so hard for the sealer's discharge, we give him the satisfaction to deliver ourselves up to Justice, willing to put up with the consequence.

I of course spoke on their behalf as well as the sealer, and they being Military men, the Officers were very glad to let them off as easy as possible. The Sergeant, he was suspended for six months, the Corporal the same, and the two privates sent to the Corrall for six months to the fort, there to do duty. Thus the whole of the affair ended and I returned home, though very much annoyed by their continual thanks for what I had done.

Thus time rolled on for upwards of four months from the day of our arrival, when news spread that a Frigate was at the heads, and a boat from her endeavoured to pass the outer Fort, when they let drive a 32-pounder across her bows, which caused her to return to the *Blond* Frigate which was her name, commanded by Commodore Mason. However they stood out to sea again, and at night made her appearance again. The Governor hearing this ordered the Military to go where the whole of the Englishmen were living and bring them to the guardhouse for the night. They did so, which caused my companions to be very uneasy, especially when they heard a Frigate was at the Heads. However, between 11 and 12 o'clock at night the Governor made his appearance. He then addressed the Englishmen:

No doubt you was alarmed at my ordering you to be confined. My reason for it was, I thought when you heard a Frigate was at the heads you would run in the forest and the whole of you would be killed. The Commodore has sent for you to go on board his vessel, to give an account of yourselves. Is it your wish to go?

They made the answer *No!*

Very well then, he said, *I will send the Commodore a letter stating I will send a boat for him and he shall be conducted to my Palace where he can have an interview with you but I will not allow another person to accompany him.*

My companions thanked him and he said:

If they force their way up I will send you all away to the interior and let the sea lions (a term they give the English sailors) *find you if they can. You will find a foreign officer as good and sound a heart within this breast* (placing his hand to it) *as any English officer that ever drew the breath of life.*

And as he said, so we found him in every respect. Commodore Mason, being aware he could not get us on board by fair means or foul, he up helm and bore away for Valparaiso. When the Governor received the news he released them all to their great satisfaction.

Months past on without any further interruption until such time as we heard from the Governor that the Courier was detained by the Indians on his return from the supreme Governor, who resides in the City, namely Santiago. This we were very sorry to hear, as we were anxious to know the result of the despatches. This news came to me in the country while I was residing in the house of the Lady Ascension. I now thought I had been a long time absent from my first Friend, Don Lopez. I came to a resolution to return, and made mention of my determination to the young widow, who took me by the hand and used all the art she was mistress of to detain me a month or two longer. I proved inflexible, yet to appease her I consented to pay her a visit as often as I possibly could. She at last consented, saying she would accompany me to Town on horseback. The distance, being three times as far by land as by water, which I was aware, we could not complete on horseback in less than two days. However I consented, and all things being got ready I took farewell of all my friends, but in particular the cholers, or slaves that tilled the ground, brought me up all standing, before I could leave them. Their grateful feelings for the kindness they had received from me caused, as it were, rivers of tears to flow from their dark, penetrating eyes, throwing themselves down on their knees before me. I could not stand this, I turned my head away, and requested as a favour from Lady Ascension a Barrel of Cyder to be divided among them. This was complyed with. We then returned to the house to mount the horses and away on my journey.

There was three of us in company, the Widow, her Son and myself, and at the moment we were going to start she said to me:

Santiago, you have entirely forgot Antionetta, the young slave.

These words brought things fresh to my memory, I cast a glance at her, and not a very pleasing one, and at the same time alighted from my horse in quest of her. She was not to be found. I galloped to the river side, crossed in the Canoe, enquired at the plantation, but got no tidings of her. Strange ideas came across me at the time. I immediately galloped back again, and found Lady Ascension very busy with a great number of her friends in search of the said Indian Lass, however she was not to be found.

We returned to our horses, remounted, and set off at full speed, until we came to a junction in the road called *The Two Brothers* or *Dos el Manos* — on account of the two brothers being Bachelors and farmers living at the corner of each road. We never uttered a word to each other for the half hour's ride until we reached the place I have mentioned. She then enquired the cause of my silence, or rather contempt. I made answer:

I know your revengeful disposition and it is my belief you have injured the unfortunate Antionetta whom you was pretending to look after.

She immediately took a gold Cruz, or cross, kissed it and declared she had not injured her, nor knew where she was. I believed her and thus ended the coolness between us. We remained there a short time and proceeded on our journey.

Nothing interesting happened on our journey and in a few words I once more entered under the friendly roof of Don Lopez, where the whole of them were transported with joy at seeing me. Lady Ascension remained with us for two days and then took her departure, with not one gleam of joy (apparently) in her countenance.

She had not been absent more than two days when I had occasion to take a walk in the evening, and when I returned it was rather late and no one was up at the House but Senora Lopez, the remainder of them were in bed. The old lady was inclined on a strow or kind of sofa, she beckoned to me and in a silent whisper thus began:

Santiago, have you heard any tidings of Antionetta?

Taking by surprise I could scarce answer the question. At last I answered *No*. She then said:

I am aware that unfortunate Indian Lass has fled from Lady Ascension's fury and there is no knowing what the consequences may be by her so doing, or whether she may not perish by her hasty flight.

I answered: *I hope not.*

Do you then follow me.

She arose, took the candlestick in her hand and introduced me to an apartment. Pointing to a bed she said:

There is Antionetta and my young daughter Narcissus sleeping together. She came here in a forlorn state and threw herself under my protection from the fury of her mistress, owing to you letting her down twice from her vengeance. Her next question was concerning yourself, fearful that you would be led into some error by her cruel temper. We will now return, and Don Lopez is not acquainted with her being here, or the cruelty of her mistress towards her. We will now retire to rest.

The Senora to her apartment and me to mine. I must own I laboured under a sleepless night and arose very early in the morning, but Don Lopez being an early riser was up before me, and was acquainted with the whole affair. He accosted me with *Good Morning.* I returned the compliment when a little conversation ensued and he said he would purchase Antionetta her freedom. During this time the whole of the family was up, and the girl was sent for — she made her appearance and appeared to be rather astonished at my being present.

Don Lopez informed her of his intentions, and asked her who her parents were. She said her father was a Cacique (a Chief) and during her father's absence another Chief invaded their territories. Her mother, striving to save her, lost her life, and she was sold as a slave to Lady Ascension, with whom she had been living four years and upwards, not knowing whether her father was alive or dead. With that she began sobbing and was obliged to leave the room. However that very morning Don Lopez went upon horseback to her Mistress and succeeded in his wishes. She would not accept anything from them for her liberty, but freely gave it to her. He returned with the news, to the joy of every one present and in particular the Indian lass herself, who would remain with Senora Lopez as servant.

Thus things ended in a very agreeable manner to all parties, and in a short time afterwards I had the satisfaction of

seeing her married to a Peon, a faller of timber who earned a very comfortable living.

Time passed on apace when we heard another Governor was to relieve our warm-hearted friend, Governor Sanchez, and in a few days he landed, a complete Nero, which he proved to be. Two days after he landed we were ordered to the palace when in our presence our friend Governor Sanchez acquainted the new Governor with the whole of our affair, and also mentioned to him that he had also wrote to head quarters concerning us on our behalf and that he had no doubt, come when it would, it would be in our favour.

I am also aware the Courier is detained by the Indians and there is no knowing for a certainty when he will be allowed to come away as it is their drinking season. Therefore I hope you will pay every attention to them as I have done, by placing dependence in them. I let them go where they please, they gave me their word they would not try to make their escape, nor have they attempted it, therefore I consider them worthy of being at large, and if I reach Valparaiso in safety I shall search into their case, represent everything to the Supreme Governor, and no doubt get them a discharge.

Chile

The new Governor said he would comply with him, but he meant in his black heart only while our friend remained a nigh witness to his conduct. However in the course of a week or two he took his departure and left us to the disposal of a *Tyrant*. His first Commencement was that the whole of us should make our appearance every evening at 6 o'clock to the officer of the Guard, for every person that passed to gaze upon us.

This looked as much like Macquarie Harbour Discipline that we determined the first slant of wind we got we would take french leave for it, and sail clear of him. With this intention I went on board a Barque to help fit her out which was at anchor about seven miles down the river, but to my astonishment the Governor sent two soldiers on board to watch my actions. This grieved me to the heart and on the Sunday I came to town to ask the advice of my friend Don Lopez. He advised me to remain quiet for a while and no doubt things would go better than I anticipated.

I took his advice and the same day went to one of my companions, John Barker, who at this time was married, and asked him what he intended to do. He said two of our carpenters were going to build a whale boat for the Governor, and at the same time they meant to make their escape in her, and to hold myself in readiness. This I was very glad to hear, but during this time they were building her an occurrence took place which we thought would afford us a good retreat.

A very large Brig named the *Ocean* arrived, and Contraband goods were found on board of her, for which reason she was to be sold, which would have ruined Captain West (a

Swede) and his family, having a wife and two children on board with him. As he expected he would be ruined, he brought a brace of splendid Pistols to John Barker to repair, to blow the brains out of the informers, but Barker put the question to him if he would not like his Brig back again. He said he would, but how was it to be done. Barker informed him he could find eight more of his companions who would take her from under the Battery or perish in the attempt. He thanked him and said:

That will do, if I cannot compromise matters with them it shall be as you say and I will heed your companions.

With this he bid Barker farewell who informed us of the whole proceedings, which made our hearts leap with joy at the idea of another chance, though in an affair of this description no quarters would be shewn on either side. Two days past. We heard nothing from Captain West, which made us think it would come to a crisis one way or the other very shortly, but to our sad misfortune the Captain got two Merchants as Bondsmen for him at £1000 each, when he was at liberty to sail when he pleased.

On the Sunday night, as he was to sail on the Monday morning, six of us took a small dinghy to go down in the middle of the night and get on board of her ready to sail in the morning with her, but fate decreed it otherwise. We got the Bar in a foaming surf and had to pull before it for our lives, which was the means of our not being able to reach the Brig. When we saw her get underweigh the next morning, three of our companions that was working on board of a sloop, swam to her and got clear away, leaving seven of us behind out of ten. We returned to town the next day and that same day I went on board the Barque at my usual labour and no questions asked me by anyone on board. Fatigued and vexed it was with very little heart I had to work.

The next day or two passed and they were getting on rapid with the Whale Boat, and in a short time they completed her, which done Sunday was the time appointed to start, but owing to some circumstance or other, they started on Saturday, Lesley, Barker, Russen, and the second mate of the Brig *Liberta*. Myself, not expecting them that night, turned into my Bunk in expectation of it being the last night, but what was my surprise, the next morning about 9 o'clock a boat with the Military came to demand me, and I was then conveyed to the Quartell. When I came there I found Lyons and the Traitor Cheshire chained together. Me and Shires was then chained together. I then give up hopes of ever regaining my liberty. The account the Tyrant of a Governor sent to the Supreme Governor would cause him to be prejudiced against his own Brother.

We had been confined about seven months, chained together like Dogs, when I was informed by a note from my friend Don Lopez that a vessel belonging to the English was coming to convey us back from whence we came. This touched me to the quick, and I was determined to make a bold finish for it. I got Shires to complain of sickness so that we should be separated. It had the desired effect, I got adrift from him and they put me on a pair of Bar Irons, the Bar coming across my instep so that I could only walk about 4 inches at a step. This I endured for seven weeks until I found an opportunity.

One day Antionetta came in to see me, and cryed very much. I begged of her not to cry, but asked her if I could trust her with a secret to assist me in making my escape:

As you seem to be very much hurt at my being a prisoner.

I could see her dark, penetrating eyes sparkle again at the bare recital. She quickly answered *Yes.*

Then go immediately and bring me a thin knife and file, and do not let a soul know what you are going to do.

Off she tript and when she was gone I thought it was hard to trust to the female sex (but I found out by experience it was only a saying, for in my travels I found them to be as true and staunch as my own sex). However she returned in to the Quartel in less than no time, with the file secreted in her long black hair and the knife up the sleeve of her gown. She gave them to me as private as possible, and with a pitiful countenance ejaculated:

Santa Maria protect you!

I thanked her, it was all I could do, situated as I was. She left me with a handkerchief to her eyes. The moment she had gone I went into the closet, notched the knife with the file and commenced, and in about three quarters of an hour I could take my irons off when I pleased. The night was fast advancing. The hour of eight approached when I was determined to make a fair wind of it out of fetters, or face the sabres of my foes.

I was sitting by the fire, surrounded by Cassadores, or horse soldiers that constituted the guard, giving them a sketch of the English Navy merely to divert them. My three fellow prisoners were there also, William Shires being the only man that knew my intention. When I heard the clock strike eight, a signal for me to be moving, as I past Shires my companion I squeezed his hand and he returned it with a farewell shake. I then passed on to the door which led into the back yard, but the sentinel stop't me. I busseled him and said I had the Sergeant's leave. He let me pass, for I had made it a regular practice for a fortnight to go out at 8 o'clock as they were relieving Guard and coming back correct, to avoid suspicion.

The moment I got into the yard I shook off my irons and reared a plank against the wall. I had no shoes on, I went back about 20 yards and on looking behind me saw the door open. I made a spring and ran to the top of the plank, sprung up and catched hold of the top of the wall, hauled myself up, ran down a veranda on the other side and jumped off, being exactly 12 feet from the ground. Strange to say I only stunned my feet, picked myself up again and made all the headway I could. The night was very dark and I was dressed all in white which was the worse for me. On going round the corner of a street a woman was standing with a lanthorn which gave a splendid light. I walked deliberately up to her and kicked it out of her hand, she screamed, I cared not, we were in darkness, that was all I wanted.

I could hear them giving sheet after me. I passed a turning and then turned short around and took the turning I passed, merely to defeat the vigilance of my pursuers. I soon found myself in a swamp when I bedaubed my white clothes with black soil, fearful they would see my white clothing in the dark, which done I hastened on my journey, crossed a farm or two and made the road. At that very moment I heard some one approaching on horseback, I soon found out they were the soldiers. I crouched down and let them pass, which done I hastened across the road, went through the bush, and soon reached the river side, when I saw a fisherman's hut and a canoe on the Beach. I then went and had great difficulty in getting her off. I let her hang on the beach by the stern and went in search of a paddle. I found one, and when in the act of picking it up the Casement flew open and a lump of a Spaniard thrust his head out. I made a blow at him and struck the Casement which frightened him to such a degree that I would venture to say he did not put his head out again until daylight.

I then crossed the river in a dreadful fog, my clothing covered with black mud, from which the cold was piercing my vital parts, and I thought, catched with the cramp as I was, all my troubles was coming to a close, and I should never again see the rising Sun. I could then hear the soldiers bawling out *Sentinels Alert!* This aroused me from my reverie. I launched the canoe adrift to prevent them knowing for a certainty where I had landed. I then jumped about, rubbing my hands and legs in hopes that the friction would cause a circulation of blood. I found relief by this movement, and then travelled into the interior.

All that I had about me was a knife in a sheath, about half a pound of Tobaccoa and 5 dollars in money, but nothing whatever to eat. I experienced a dismal cold night, but early the next morning I saw a Boy driving some Cows along, and in looking ahead I saw a farm House, and to my surprise found I was on a farm. However I made my way up to the House, when an elderly female requested me to come in. I did so, and set down, when in a short time she placed before me some boiled milk, bread and butter. This to me was a treat for I was both fatigued and hungry. After I had satisfied the cravings of nature, my kind hostess asked me where I had escaped from. I informed that I ran away from a French Whaler that was at anchor under the Corral fort. She smiled and made answer:

You cannot deceive me, Santiago, do you know Carmaletta Rey?

I replied *Yes.*

That is my daughter, she is married to a young man called Cockney Tom.

She saw me start at the name when she said:

Do not be alarmed, for I do not allow him near my premises, and it is my wish for you to stop here and I will wash your clothing for you, and you can start in the morning clean and comfortable.

I was very thankful for her kindness and consented to stop, and I found myself very comfortable and greatly refreshed when I put my clean things on the next morning very early. It was my wish (having money about me) to pay her for her kindness and trouble, but she would not accept of it. I then took my departure and proceeded on my journey.

I walked the whole of that day, when towards evening I threw myself down and in a very short time I was asleep, and did not awake until the middle of the night, wet through with the dew from the heavens. I got up and walked about, for I found my limbs benumbed, which caused me to travel on until morning daylight, when I observed some beautiful Indian Corn. I walked through about 100 acres of it, and in fact, in its raw state made a hearty meal of it. The moment I reached the extremity of the Corn I saw a beautiful Farm House, and necessity compelled me to steal from there a Poncho, or Mantle, to keep me from the inclemency of the weather in the night.

I immediately struck in towards the mountains with my prize. When about 2 o'clock in the day I made the mountain, struck onto a path, travelled on with all possible speed, and to my sorrow, late in the evening I found I had struck into a beaten track occasioned by cattle continually passing to and thro, which brought me to the same spot I had started from. Fatigued with walking and vexed at my disappointment I threw myself down on the grass, not even concealing myself, rolled the Poncho around me and very soon fell into a sound sleep. I awakened in the middle of the night, arose and shook the dew off the mantle, walked about for an hour or so, and then retired beneath the huge branches of a sarrifax tree, and towards morning sunk into a sound repose, but to my astonishment a little after daylight I felt something tugging at the mantle that covered me.

I immediately sprung upon my feet, when I saw a young man of robust appearance stand before me with a knife in his hand, and demanded the mantle as his father's property. I gave it to him in the hopes it would silence him but he was not content, he said I must go with him as a prisoner. This aroused me, I knew he was too clever for me with a knife, so I parlayed with him until I got an opportunity and seized a piece of the limb of a tree, which he perceiving made a rush at me, at which he received a blow which nearly unshp't his truck and caused him to give a lee lurch. I followed him up and brought him to the ground, took the knife and Poncho from him, and when he came to himself and able to walk, I made him Pilot me over the Mountain and put me in the direct road for the Imperial near the Sea Coast, and as nigh as I can judge, about 3 o'clock PM we were at the two cross roads. He told me one led to the Imperial and the other to Conception. He looked very pitiful at me with the streaks of blood that had dried on his forehead, and begged very hard for his knife. I threw it from me a good distance, ordered him to go and pick it up and upon the peril of his life not to come in pursuit of me. He thanked me and made his exit. Thus far I got rid of a troublesome Customer without sustaining any injury. I then travelled, though weak in body, as fast as I could for Conception, a beautiful little village. I travelled to that excess up a hill to gain the level, expecting my pursuers would be after me, that when I gained the summit I was completely exhausted.

I went and sat down on the bank, and had not been there more than ten minutes when five horse soldiers sprung from the top of the hill I had but a few minutes ascended, and sprang alongside of me. Their sabres were quivering over my head and, had it not been for the Sergeant, I should have lost my life, for the Tyrant of a Governor had issued out orders to take very little trouble with me, I would answer him dead as well as alive. But the Sergeant ordered I should be placed on a horse and my feet lashed with a lassoe under the animal's belly.

This was done, and in this state they conveyed me to the first village, when I found I was getting very ill with the Dissentry. They certainly behaved very kind to me and the remainder of the night I slept in a very good bed, with a soldier inside the same apartment doing duty, being relieved every two hours. Thus the night past, daylight made its appearance and I arose to breakfast. There was a great number of females looking at me and sympathetic with me in my unfortunate situation. However we started about 9 o'clock, and owing to my being unwell I was not lashed to the horse.

We rode on until about 4 o'clock when we arrived at a Farm House along the side of the river where we had some refreshment. The canoe was then in readiness to convey us across the river. The five soldiers got into her with all their horses' gear, and the horses standing in the water to start with the canoe. All being ready I was standing on the Bank about seven feet above the Canoe when I was called to come into her. I jumped from the bank of the river in to the gunwale of the canoe with the reviving hope of capsizing them, not caring if I drowned them all to make my escape, but all was in vain, and fortunately for me they were so blind as not to suspect my design.

When we reached the opposite shore we all mounted again and a little after dusk we arrived at another farm house where a large pair of stocks were kept. I had some supper brought me, and afterwards I was placed in the stocks. I had not been in them more than half an hour when the Cholers that was placed there to watch me made a fire which, being so near to my feet, it put me in great pain. I ordered them to shift it further away, they gave me no answer. Being enraged by the heat of the fire so close to my feet I took up a large stone and threw it with all the violence I could among the three of them, and knocked one of them kicking. The alarm was give, they rushed in upon me and confined as I was, they thrashed me with the broad part of their sabres, until I was black and blue. Confined as I was I could not help myself, which nearly caused my aching heart to break. They did not cease at this, they fastened a cord above the ankle of each leg, and then hauled me up as far as they could get them through the stocks to two beams that went across above their heads, leaving me as it were nearly lying upon my shoulders. In this excruciating Torture I remained until morning.

Sleep was an entire stranger to me that night and when they cast me adrift I could not move. In the morning early the Sergeant came in, who appeared to be an entire stranger to their cruel proceedings. He asked me if I was any better. I looked at him and made answer:

Better! How could you expect me to be better, or even alive, after the cruel treatment you have practiced on me the whole night?

He was struck with astonishment. When I related the facts of the case, he ordered the eight Cholers and the four Military men to be conducted into the Town of Valdivia before him, and to be confined for cruelty until he made his appearance against them. I could not travel that day, being so sore after their ill treatment, however I was pretty well recovered by the next day to proceed on my journey.

A Choler of confidence had me in charge to convey me to Valdivia. We started, having a horse each. When we came to a very long mountain we both rode up until we nearly reached the summit, when I alighted from my horse which followed me like a dog. The place where the horses and mules travel was so much worn away that they were up to their knees every step they took. The pass was not more than three feet wide, so that when the horse was ascending in the centre he had very little room on either side of him. But outside of those holes, close to the precipice of more than 300 feet of a fall, there was a small pass for the travellers to walk on, and the Choler, to make himself appear a courageous fellow in my sight, actually rode his horse on this said critical path.

The thoughts of their cruelty to me came fresh in my memory. I was resolved to be revenged and get my liberty if I could at the same time. I then went to the tail of his horse, catched hold of it and, as I thought, with a sudden jerk hurl him and the horse down the precipice. I did my best by suddenly snatching the quarter of his horse towards the precipice, one of the horse's hoofs I got over the brink by the sudden twist I gave him. No sooner did the Choler find his horse giving way then he drove the rowel of the spur that was on his right heel into the side of the horse with such violence that he fairly lifted him clean out of the eminent danger he was in. Nor could he account for it in any other way than he thought his horse slip't, no suspicion fell on me, as I thought, for it was never hinted to me as much.

All went on well afterwards and when we reached the plains on the other side of the mountain, we fell in with a Lieutenant and five soldiers that had been in pursuit of me. He said he was very sorry that I was taken, which was all the consolation he could give me. We proceeded on our journey, and towards evening was ushered into an apartment in the Governor's House where he was lolling in an easy chair surrounded by officers.

The question to me was: *What caused you to run away?*

My answer was precisely thus: *Two reasons I had for so doing: first, the cruel treatment and oppression of a Tyrant like yourself, secondly, with the hope of obtaining my Liberty.*

The Governor then made answer: *Take him to the Blacksmith's shop and see that a pair of Bar Irons is welded on his legs, and tomorrow I will order him to be shot in the Public square.*

I was quite indifferent as to whether he put into execution or not, for I was actually tired of my life. I was then taken to the blacksmith's shop, ordered to stand upon a large Anvil, the Irons were put upon me, and a piece of iron, red hot, lifted hissing from the fire, was placed in the end of the bar and actually welded in, to prevent the Bar from slipping through. There were many young people, both male and female, pitying me and many among them crying, expecting I would be shot in the morning with the irons on me.

I was conducted back to the Quartel and separated from my companions. That night several of the inhabitants came to console me in my unfortunate situation, but I needed none, I was quite resigned to my fate, for I expected the Governor would act up to his word. However, towards the morning Padre Rosa came to me and informed me himself and his Brother priests, and several females of distinction had been to the Governor, and they found him a long time inflexible:

When at last he consented to spare your life and requested me to be the Bearer of the news, which I have done with great pleasure, and during your confinement here I shall send your meals regular to you from my table.

I returned my sincere and grateful thanks for his kindness, and to all those who had been so kind as to use their influence in my behalf. He passed his Benediction on me, shook hands with me and departed. About 7 o'clock that morning, Padre Rosa was as good as his word: he sent me a comfortable breakfast but I could not eat a bit of it, my appetite had entirely deserted me. On or about the same time the Governor made his appearance and informed I had to thank my numerous friends for being then alive as I richly merited Death for absconding. I informed him I had thanked them in the strongest manner my grateful feeling would allow me, but as for him, I would not thank him for prolonging a life like mine, a life of misery, and in particular he, the Governor, being the chief cause of it by his Oppression. He cast a fierce glance at me and then left me to myself.

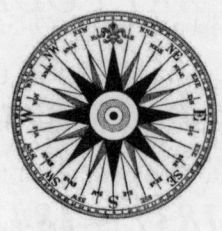

End Part Three

PART FOUR

Return to Van Diemens Land

1837 ~ 1842

backs, and at this time they were getting ~~very~~
~~better~~, at this time I got pen ink and paper with a
view to write a letter to my friends and while meditating
upon my truly unfortunate situation those few
lines came into my head ———

How wretched is an Exile's state of mind
When not one gleam of hope on earth remain
Though grief worn down with servile chains confined,
And not one friend to sooth his heartfelt pain.
Too true I know that man was made to mourn
A heavy portion's fallen to my lot
With anguish full my aching heart is torn
Far from my friends by all the world forgot,
The feathered race with splendid plumage gay
Extend their throats with a discordant sound
With Liberty they spring from spray to spray
While I a wretched Exile gaze around
Farewell my Sister, Aged Parents dear,
Ere long my glass of life will cease to run
In silence drop a sympathetic tear
For your Unhappy. Exiled. long lost Son;
O Cease my troubled aching heart to beat
Since happiness so far from thee has flea
Haste, haste unto your silent cold retreat
In clay cold earth to mingle with the Dead
    I had scarcely finished it; when a Soldier

PART FOUR

Return to Van Diemens Land

1837 ~ 1838

hus days, weeks and months rolled on, when at last orders came: myself and three others were to be removed down the river to be lodged on board the *Basilisk* Schooner, tender to the *Blond* Frigate, commanded by Commodore Mason. This took place when the inhabitants was taking their siesta in the afternoon so that we should not be disturbed by them.

We reached the vessel at dark that evening and the first person I recognised on board was the Tyrant of a Governor, the cause of a great part of my misery. Without further hesitation I unship't a belaying pin and struck at him in the hight of my passion, with an intention of having revenge for his past cruelties. The blow glided from his head and struck him on the collar bone which caused him to shriek, and before I could repeat the blow my arm was arrested by the Quartermaster and the belaying pin taken from me. I was ordered below with the other three, being somewhat satisfied that I had left a mark on him to return to Valdivia with.

The next morning the Schooner got underweigh and in three days and nights brought up in Valparaiso. The commander of the *Basilisk* heard on his arrival that the *Blond* Frigate had sailed for Calloa, the Capital sea Port of Peru. Owing to this, the next day we got underweigh and shaped our course for Calloa. We called in at Concepcion, a small sea port, remained there three days and then got underweigh again for our place of destination which we reached in safety, and I have further to state that the officers and seamen of the *Basilisk* treated us with humane kindness, pitying our unfortunate situation, for which I returned them my sincere and greatful thanks.

We were then drafted aboard the Friggate, ordered between decks and put into shackels, or Bar Irons, between two guns, opposite the gun room on the starboard side of the Deck. We only had one enemy aboard, which was the first Lieutenant, but the humanity of the second Lieutenant made up for it, and I had the fortune to find two bluejackets on board that had been my shipmates, and a sailor's heart always being open to a shipmate in distress, they relieved me in every sense of the word.

A Last and Desperate Chance

We remained in Calleo some few days and then got underweigh to return to Valparaiso. On our return we put into Concepcion and there I contrived to make my escape. I made it known to my companion, William Shires, who was to be depended on, but he could not swim, and it was impossible for me to get off the bar without the other two of my fellow prisoners knowing of it, therefore my companion thought it advisable to sound them on the subject. They consented. On Saturday night was the appointed time to make the trial. On the afternoon of the night we were to go, I ordered them to go forward in the head, and during the time they were absent I contrived to oval the shakels, so that we could slip them when occasion required. We had agreed on account of Shires not being able to swim to get him on shore between us, but he, being rather fearful of the water, he said:

I should be sorry to be the means of being a check on your liberty, Jimmy. I care not for the other two, we know they are scoundrels, yet we cannot avoid their knowing it. Therefore there can be no dependence to be placed in them. When I am overboard they may desert us, and I should be too heavy for you, which may be the means of your being taken and them two get clear off. I will stop behind, it will be far better for me to die an ignominious death than the both of us. My only request is that, should you get clear off, you will not forget to see Catalina, my wife, and also my little Boy, and be a friend to them, for I shall never see them more.

He turned away from me before I could make an answer, with his eyes full of tears. This was almost too much from me, especially to part from a man, a friend, who had risked his life with me, but I came to a determination should I escape I would be a

93

friend to his Wife, and a Father to his only child, Bernado. However night came on, a clock calm, the moon spreading its lustre around, which occasioned the night to be as light as the day, which was to be disadvantage. I was eagerly watching my oppertunity, when I awoke Lions, and the cowardly rascal began [snoring] and I ascertained he was not asleep. The Traitor Cheshire was wide awake at the time. Finding no one was inclined to go I took hold of my Companion Shires hand and took, as I thought, a last farewell shake while he was asleep.

I then placed my pea jacket along the bed (for we were all sleeping on the deck) to make it appear, should the sentinel look over, that I was sleeping with my head under the clothes. Which done I looked around me and found the Marine that was keeping watch over us was washing on the other side of the gun. I then crawled away upon my hands and knees and got to the midship port, removed some things that were in my way and got into the main Chains. I was compelled to keep close to the vessel's side as I could use the shade and hear the voice of the sentinel and Quarter Master on deck. I sneaked along the side of the vessel as well as I could to reach the Mizzen Chains, for I wished to get out of the hearing of the Sentinel and Quarter Master.

I had scarce got my foot upon the Mizzen Chains when the Marine presented a pistol at my head and ordered me to come in board. Of course I could do no other, for there were two boats swinging to the guess-warp alongside. Had I have jumped overboard, it being as light as day, I should have been taken. However I came in, and went to my bed in a state of despair, and I was aroused from my reverie by a sailor touching me, telling me I was betrayed by one of my Companions shaking the irons to attract the sentinel's attention. He looked over and found I was missing, which caused me to be taken.

However, in the morning we were ordered upon deck, one at a time. Cheshire declared he knew nothing about it, Lyons the same, but when William Shires was called he said he was equally guilty with me, and willing to share the punishment with me, and that the two scringing hounds that denied any knowledge of it also knew about it, and was to have gone, but their cowardly hearts would not allow them. They were ordered to stand on one side when the first Lieutenant sent for me and asked the reason I had tried to make my escape. I informed him that I thought I had been a prisoner long enough, and knowing I was innocent of any crime I considered I had an undoubted right to escape if I could, and that he could give orders to the sentinel that, if he saw me away from the Guns where I was confined, to shoot me, and by the same rule, if I saw a sentinel off his guard I should go overboard, in spite of fate, let the consequence be what it would.

When Commodore Mason made his appearance on deck and said:

Let the man go below, it is natural the man would try to make his escape, and we must endeavour to keep him. If they are guilty of the crime they are charged with they are to be pitied, and if not, then the case is very aggravating to them. Go down below now!

Return to Van Diemens Land

We went down below decks and were put in irons and in a few days after we got underweigh for Valparaiso which we reached in safety. We were then drafted on board the *North Star*, eighty and twenty gun ship bound for England, and in May 10th 1836 we sailed from Valparaiso and experienced dreadful weather under close-reefed topsails surrounded with icebergs, being seven weeks before we could weather Cape Horn. We touched at Rio de Janiero, and in the latter end of October we were guarded on board the *Leviathan* Prison Hulk at Portsmouth.

The next morning we were conveyed aboard the *Brittania* guard ship, and there we were handcuffed from Friday afternoon till Monday morning, two and two, upon two gratins, with four marines over us, and a man for the express purpose of cutting our provisions up in small pieces, when we had to convey it to our mouths the best way we could. We were not even allowed to go to the head without a lump of a marine being lashed to each of us. However, on Monday morning we were ushered into the stateroom before Captain Dundas and several officers, and went through a kind of private examination. Captain Dundas appeared willing to release me but said it was out of his power.

We were then sent back to the Hulk where we went through a thorough repair, clean washed and close shaved, and the rigging they gave me to put on fitted me like a purser's shirt upon a handspike. However a great quantity of old Gangers came to see if they could recognize any of us, also Captains of different Hulks, and not one of them knew any of us, and in the month of December, being the 23rd day of that month, we embarked on board the *Sarah* Barque, commanded by Captain White, and on the 24th set sail for Van Diemens Land.

The moment we got into the Channel nearly all of the prisoners were sick. I then exerted myself in assisting them all I could, and kept the Prison clean from filth, for which I got great praise from the Doctors and Officers on board, and my irons were struck directly. Having a loose leg I could go aloft and be of good assistance to Captain White. This passed on for more than one month and all hands were in good health on board, when a wretched Conspiracy, got up by two foul fiends, blasted all my hopes and made me a wretched object.

Thus then it was. The Captain and Doctor had received an information that the ship was to be taken and all were to be put to death with the exception of those who fought for their liberty. I did not know a word of this, when in the morning the Doctor and Captain called me on the Quarter Deck, ordered me to put my legs on a block and ordered a man to iron me. I was astonished at this, for I knew I had not committed myself. However, at 8 o'clock, all hands were called upon Deck and the number that was selected out as Conspirators were sixty. There was English, Irish, Canadians, Spanish and Italians, and also a poor French Sailor that was on board did not escape the Villains. However the first that was called out for punishment was my Companion, William Shires. He wanted to know what it was for. The Doctor would not give him any satisfaction, so they gave him four dozen with a log line, which nearly killed him.

They then called me. I commenced buttoning up my jacket, determined to have a bit of a dust on the Deck unless I knew what it was for. I informed him, the Doctor, that I was a free man and that he would find it out as soon as we arrived at Van Diemens Land. Though I was then a prisoner under his Charge and in Chains, I informed him, he could punish me if he thought proper, without rhyme or reason, and he must put up with the consequence when we arrived at our place of destination. My motive for this was to endeavour to find out who those monsters were that had raised a plot of this description. It answered my wish when, lo and behold, who should step forward but Charles Lyon and William Cheshire that escaped in the *Frederick* brig with us, and declared I was going to head 12 Canadians to rush the Quarter Deck and slaughter all before me.

Knowing my innocence I stood nearly petrified, and before I could recover my surprise I was seized by the soldiers and seamen, lashed to a gratin, and to that degree until the blood hoosed from the parts where the lashings went round different parts of my person, and a lump of a black fellow flogged me across the lines and every other part of my Body until my head sank on my breast. As for the quantity of lashes I cannot say, for I would not give them the satisfaction to scringe to it, until nature gave way through exhaustion and knew no more about it until I was cast adrift.

I then gazed around me and saw my Companion Shires who was as unfortunate as myself. All this time they were flogging the men those two miscreants were pointing out, nor did they cease flogging till 7 bells, half past eleven o'clock, being upwards of three hours inflicting of torture. Myself and my Companion were ordered below and put into one of the Berths below, fitted up by the Doctor's orders so it would scarcely contain us. Our feet were chained together, our hands behind us, our bodies lacerated in a shocking manner, bleeding profusely. The heat of the place added to our missery, and what was worse than all, the two miscreants that were once our Companions, who had plunged us into this missery by their false accusation, were placed as Sentinels over us, to see that we got neither water, food nor Tobbaccoa given to us by any of our fellow prisoners. Alas, who could describe my feelings, no person in existence, it was past description. That was the time, my gentle reader, I craved for Death to alleviate my tortured feelings, and when describing this part of my narrative my feelings are harrowed up to such a pitch that revenge is uppermost in my thoughts.

For three long weeks we were confined in this cruel manner, that I began to suspect at last we should remain in this Torture all the passage, but the Doctor visiting us one morning (and we having the appearance of anatomys more than living beings) he ordered us to be released. His order was obeyed: certainly I must say it was a happy releasement. The Doctor then sent for me and asked me whether I was guilty or not. I answered him, as he considered himself a Judge he ought to have proved it before he tortured me in the manner he had. I then took up the Bible and swore a solemn oath in his presence: I neither knew hand, act, or part in the affair, nor did I think anything of the kind was to take place, but that he, the Doctor, would find out the two miscreants had only used this plan with a view to make it appear to the passengers that they had saved their lives, and the lives of all on board, so that by this stratagem (and a most cruel one it was) their lives will be spared when they reach their place of destination.

I then turned around upon my heels and returned to my Companion, when we got some warm water and washed each others backs, and at this time they were getting better. At this time I got pen, ink and paper with a view to write a letter to my friends, and while meditating upon my truly unfortunate situation, these few lines came into my head:

How wretched is an Exile's state of mind
When not one gleam of hope on earth remain
Through grief worn down, with servile chains confined,
And not one friend to soothe his heartfelt pain.

Too true I know that man was made to mourn,
A heavy portion's fallen to my lot.
With anguish full my aching heart is torn,
Far from my friends by all the world forgot.

The feathered race with splendid plumage gay
Extend their throats with a discordant sound,
With Liberty they spring from spray to spray
While I a wretched Exile gaze around.

Farewell my Sister, aged Parents dear,
Ere long my glass of life will cease to run.
In silence drop a sympathetic tear
For your Unhappy, Exiled, long-lost son.

O cease, my troubled, aching heart, to beat,
Since happiness so far from thee has fled
Haste, haste unto your silent cold retreat
In clay cold earth to mingle with the Dead.

I had scarcely finished it when a Soldier Officer and two of his men rushed upon me exclaiming:

I have you at last, you scoundrel!

And snatched the paper out of my hand, but when he read the contents he waved his hands for the two soldiers to go on deck. He looked steadfastly at me, asked me if the lines were my Composition. I answered *Yes*, and also my genuine feelings were summed up in the said few lines. He exclaimed: *I feel sorrow for you, I pitty you.* I asked him why he rushed upon me in the manner he did. He said Cheshire had given an information to the Doctor that you were writing on small pieces of Paper, and sending them round to different individuals to persuade the prisoners to rush and take the ship. I asked him his opinion of the miscreant that gave the information. He answered:

I believe him to be a perjured villain and on that account I will stand your friend.

I thanked him when he left me, taking with him the few verses I had composed. In about half an hour I was ordered into the dispensary before the Doctor, the Captain and the Lieutenant of the Military and also the Chief Mate, and Captain of the ship. Several questions were put to me concerning the capture of the Brig *Frederick*. I denyed having any knowledge of it, for certain reasons of my own. They asked me if Lyons and Cheshire were ever my companions, my answer was *No*. The Captain said it was very strange they should own me and I would not own them. I made answer:

When we arrive at our place of destination then you will find whether I am wright or wrong.

It may appear strange that I persisted in this falsehood, therefore I will give you one reason. I suspected, had I informed them I was the man they represented me, they would have looked sharper after me and prevented my making an escape, for it was my intention, as soon as we made the Head Land of Hobart Town to endeavour to make my escape, as I knew every Creek and Corner in it. This then was the principal cause of my persisting in the falsehood.

But to proceed. After this interview I was allowed a little more liberty in the vessel, still my actions were watched very narrowly. Everything went on well until we were within a week's sail of our destined port, when Cheshire (the promoter of all evil) was taken before the Doctor upon the Quarter Deck, and there accused by two men of endeavouring to persuade them to swear with him that another Conspiracy was in contemplation, and if they would be staunch he would answer that both of them would get a ticket of leave when they arrived in Hobart Town. They asked Cheshire how they were to act. He answered, they must swear they overheard me, my Companion, and several Canadians contriving a plan to get through the dispensary, force the bulk head and get into the Cabin and then the ship would be our own. This was the declaration of the two men, who would not be biased by this perfidious villain, Cheshire.

This last act of his had entirely overthrown all the good he had considered he had done for himself by the first false information that he gave, and was the means of turning the passengers and every individual in the ship against him. The Doctor then ordered him to be placed on a form between Decks, not allowed to speak to an individual the remainder of the voyage, with a sentinel over him, and if he disobeyed the orders were to run him through. To see the destroyer of my happiness and Traitor withall ensnared in his own trap that he set for me and others, gave me great satisfaction, knowing that it would be the means also of him sharing the same fate with me, be it what it would. To exult in a person's downfall is quite foreign to my nature, but pardon me, on such an occasion as this I could not avoid it, as he has proved himself a Monster in human shape.

After this had taken place the Doctor began to suspect he had cruely treated me and my Companion William Shires wrongfully, and also the French Sailor belonging to the ship, who ever since the first information had been kept in irons and brutally treated by Captain and men, but they dare not take him out of irons, fearful he would put the case in the Lawyers' hands at Hobart Town and enter an action against them for false imprisonment and cruelty. Thus, to save themselves, they were obliged to get some of the prisoners who were bad enough, to declare that the French Sailor asked them to assist in the taking of the ship, which would justify the Captain and the Doctor for their cruelty towards him.

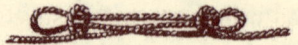

In March, 28th day, 1837 we came to an anchor in Hobart Town Harbour, named The Cove, it being early in the morning. About 12 o'clock Captain Foster, the Police Magistrate, came on board when, to the astonishment of all present, I was recognized as one of the men that captured the Brig *Frederick*. We were then conveyed on shore and the French Sailor with us, he being also in irons the same as we were. I felt for him from my heart, his haggard appearance occasioned by fretting caused him to have a ghastly appearance. He held his head down, the only foreigner among us. I knew he was innocent. All those things rushed into my mind all at once, and at that very moment the crowd was so great which caused Cheshire to come close to me. I seized him by the throat and hurled him over my hip and would have kicked his brains out, but was prevented by the Police.

We however soon reached the prison when myself and my Companion were separated from the other two. The next morning we went to the Police office and were sworn to — Cheshire tried his last effort even in the Police office to save himself, but Captain Foster was too shrude a gentleman to allow him to escape, and also informed him that an approver was not required, and to prepare himself to share the same fate with his companions. I could not avoid ejaculating *Thank you Sir!* which caused the whole of the Gentlemen that were in the office to turn around and look at me. When the Magistrate asked me why I had thanked him I replied because I saw he was administering Justice by not allowing an approver in the Case.

I am guilty and willing to put up with the consequences, and if I die for it, it will not be for a dishonorable offence.

The Gentlemen that were present said they were of my opinion. We were then returned to prison, fully Committed to take our trial for piracy on His Majesty's High Seas, and on the 26th day of April 1837 I was tried for the said offence — the Trial commencing at 10 o'clock in the morning and we were found guilty of Piracy at half past 10 at night. Irons of 35lb weight were fastened on my legs, and then put into a cell with my companion in misfortune. Expecting our days were numbered we comforted each other as well as our situation would allow, and had not the Colony been under the Government of (the humane) Sir John Franklin I should not have been alive to have given this small Narative of my life. Woe to us had the blood thirsty Arthur have ruled, as the vessel was christened after his son's name, *Frederick*.

I was two years and four months confined in Hobart Town Gaol in irons, when orders came we were to be forwarded to Norfolk Island, where Tyranny and Cruelty was in its vigour. We never received any sentence from the court but I found out when I reached there it was for life. One Major Bumbry was Commandant when I landed and I saw a specimen of his cruelty the moment I landed. A man was being dragged before him, with irons on, he could scarce crawl in, and before he could reach the office he ordered him 50 lashes without even inquiring into the case. I then considered him a second Nero.

105

I had not been there long when a Major Rian succeeded Bumbry and O the difference in the race of men: he proved himself to be as much the father to the poor exiles as Bumbry did the Brute. Things went on very well at this time, and whenever Major Rian would converse with the prisoners he would inform them that one Captain Maconochie would soon make his appearance among us, and that he was a better and a kinder Commandant than himself. This struck us with umasement!

When at last he arrived, as a proof of his Humanity the Gallows that used to stare us in the face was by his orders cut down and burned, a sure sign of a good feeling. His whole study has been to make us prisoners comfortable, and by Kind and Humane treatment to work a reformation in us. It has had the desired effect on many refractory Characters that could not be ruled by harsh and cruel treatment. I speak for myself and five more young men that would rush upon the points of Bayonets to obtain our liberty previous to Captain Maconochie's arrival on the Island. We have given our words not to abscond with a Boat, nor allow her to be taken under any circumstances.

The Captain has placed dependence in us, and we have proved to him and to all the officers on the island that our Commandant's Humanity has brought us to a sense of our duty, never to lose the only thing an exile doth possess, *his word*; where harsh treatment and Tyranny would drive a man to despair and compel him to break a thousand words to get away from it.

Thus you will find, my gentle reader, after all my trials and troubles I am safe moored at Norfolk Island, under a Commandant that alleviates the sufferings of the wretched Exile, and I now live in hopes by my good conduct of once more being a member of good Society.

Concluded

JAMES PORTER

Records at the time of the Seizure of the Frederick, 1834

Height 5'2" Age 29. Brown Hair, brown eyes. Blind left eye, two scars on forehead, dimple on chin, mole front of neck, scar left side of neck. Pugilists on left Arm.
Father and Mother at Grange Road, weigher at Customs House.
Trade: Beer Machine Maker. Last lived at Elephant & Castle.
Tried for House Breaking Kingston March 1823 Transported Life.
Gaol Report very bad Character bad behaved. Hulk report disorderly.

Arrived VDL January 1824 No. 324 per *Asia*.

April 22 1824: Suspicion of Stealing a Cask of Butter & having no lodgings.

May 22 1824: Absconding. 100 lashes.

August 31 1826: Absconding & being found on board the *Sydney Packet* with intent to escape from the Colony. 50 lashes & 6 Months Chain Gang.

January 26 1827: Robbing a Sailor, dismissed for want of evidence.

July 24 1827: Out after hours and abusive & insolent to Private Kelly. Reprimanded.

March 1 1827: Absent all night. Reprimanded.

June 10 1828: Making use of the Government Boat to his own advantage & taking men down the River. 25 lashes.

October 5 1828: Stealing a Boat and Two Oars. Not Guilty.

Nov 19 1828: Stealing 70 Boards. 7 Years Transportation.

January 30 1830: Absconding while under Sentence. Sentenced to be Hanged. Commuted to 7 Years Transportation at Macquarie Harbour.

July 11 1832: Not taking care of some Tobacco. 25 Lashes.

Nov 7 1832: Leaving his work. 3 Weeks on Bread and Water.

Dec 18 1832: Absconding into the Woods. 100 Lashes, 6 Months in Irons and 2 Months imprisonment in Gaol at Night.

January 13 1834: Piratically seized the Brig *Frederick* at Macquarie Harbour.

Records from 1837 to 1853 Hobart Norfolk & Sydney

Age 33. Height 5'2" Brown Hair & Brown Eyes, two scars on forehead, two on side of neck. Crucifix on right arm. Pugilists, a Sailor and Anchor on left arm.

April 26 1837:		Tried for Piracy on His Majesty's High Seas. Sentenced to be Hanged.
August	*1839:*	Pardoned on Condition of being Transported to Norfolk Island for Life.
May	*1841:*	Assisted in saving some of the Officers of the settlement and other persons who were upset in a Boat returning from the *Governor Phillip*. Sentence reduced to 14 Years.
October	*1842:*	Supplying with Water a Brig in Distress. Sentence reduced to Seven Years.
May	*1843:*	Returned to Sydney. Recommended that the remainder of his Sentence be Remitted.
October	*1844:*	Sent to Newcastle. Absenting. Seven Days Gaol.
February	*1845:*	Disobedience. Seven Days in the Cells
April	*1845:*	Assault. 14 Days in the Cells.
April	*1845:*	Gave information leading to the seizure of an illicit still.
June	*1845:*	Sent to Sydney and made Wardsman at Hyde Park Barracks.
January 22 1846:		Granted Ticket of Leave.
Feb 11	*1846:*	Stealing a Bundle. Ticket of Leave Cancelled. Two Months House of Corrections.
April b	*1846:*	Sent to Newcastle
May 18	*1846:*	Absent from District. Supposed to have left the Colony in the *Sir John Byng* Brig from Newcastle to Wellington, N.Z.
December 1853:		Struck off Records.

And that is the last we hear of Jimmy Porter. But I doubt he stayed in New Zealand, too close to Britain's influence. I would like to think he chose to return to Chile where he had friends, lovers, and indeed family, and where he thought of himself as a 'patriot'.

R.D.

An AFTERWORD

By Hamish Maxwell-Stewart

James Porter entered the records of Van Diemens Land as an ordinary convict. Police Number 324 James Porter per *Asia* 1824, 19 years age, blind in his left eye. He was actually 23, and his blind eye is a detail not noted in his description in 1838 nor featured in any of his writings. Identity can be more slippery than identification, less set. James Porter was to prove a man of many sides, an elusive figure constantly evading police number 324, even when he was in custody.

Seven years after the trial of 1837, Porter's story was serialised in a Scottish newspaper, the *Fife Herald,* as *'The Convict',* the adventures of one James Connor. Told as a romantic saga, it was prefaced with assurances of authenticity (the convict's name went unremarked):

> *SIR, - Having become possessed of some MS notes written by a person named James Connor, a native of Dublin, giving a sketch of his sufferings in New South Wales, and in which there are a few stirring incidents, I have transcribed them. Should you consider the facts worthy of publication, you are welcome to them. Cupat 1844*   *W.?*

Over the next thirteen editions of the *Fife Herald,* Connor's trials and tribulations unfolded. The narrative's opening pitch was crude but effective: generous dollops of carefully connected sex and 'savages' in the first two episodes. Once the readers of the *Fife Herald* had finished the serialized version, they were offered a bound, slightly truncated version. Two years later another edition appeared in Montreal Canada under the title *Recollections of a Convict and Miscellaneous Pieces by Y-Le.* With an account that can be found in the Colonial Secretary's Correspondence in Hobart in 1837, a version published in the 1838 *Hobart Almanack,* and a further one from Norfolk Island in 1842, there are in total six versions of one convict narrative.

In the earliest version of the Porter narrative, written while he sat in a condemned cell in the Hobart Town gaol, the narrator was clearly writing to save his life. He has left us an eyewitness account of how the *Frederick* was taken, but is he to be trusted? If Porter can make people see him as misled rather than villainous, sympathy might tilt in his direction and he might avoid the gallows tree. He will tell a story of mutiny in which other men dash about menacingly. Not my doing, Porter says, I was in the wrong place at the wrong time. In November 1837 Porter completed his self portrait as an innocuous bit-player caught up in a drama of someone else's devising, and he sent the manuscript to the Colonial Secretary, intent on making a good impression.

At some stage the existence of this convict narrative came to the attention of William Gore Elliston. Son of an actor and theatre manager, Elliston went from his studies at Cambridge to manage the reading room in Lymington, then from the spa town to London where he managed the Royal Theatre in Drury Lane (where incidentally Porter's life of crime began!), and in 1830 from London to Van Diemens Land. About the time Porter went on trial, Elliston acquired the colony's most widely distributed newspaper, the *Hobart Town Courier*. He had borrowed heavily and needed to make money. Porter needed a pardon. The colony had been abuzz with stories of the mutineers and their remarkable trial. As a tale of suspense and escape, Porter's narrative had lurid appeal that later shifted into a register of sex and violence for the readers of Fife. Elliston included Porter's narrative in the *Hobart Town Almanack and Van Diemens Land Annual*. The interests of convict and newspaper proprietor converge in the condemned man's last words:

> We were placed upon our trial before the Chief Justice of the Colony at Hobart Town, in Van Diemens Land, and found guilty, and sentenced to be hanged; but which we have every reason to believe will be commuted to transportation for life and our case has gone home for opinion of the English Judges.

The legal pyrotechnics and doubts surrounding the case were enough to cause Chief Justice Pedder some concern, and the colonial government prevaricated for two years as it wondered what to do. Elliston's publication of Porter's account played an important part in prompting a decision. Porter's strategy for narrating himself out of the noose succeeded brilliantly. In May 1839 the condemned men learned that they were to be pardoned on condition of transportation for life. All four were shipped off to Norfolk Island.

On Norfolk Island James Porter wrote the narrative, published for the first time in this book, about the mutiny on the *Frederick* with himself at the centre as swashbuckling hero in the mould of Errol Flynn and just as irresistible to the ladies. This figure of derring-do, created ironically under the gaze of Alexander MacConochie, a commandant experimenting with convict narrative as convict reform, would captivate audiences on the other side of the world. It is this Norfolk Island narrative that the *Fife Herald* and Montreal editors recast for their readers, although it is not clear who was responsible for delivering a version of Porter's tale to the office of the *Fife Herald*.

It was not just to be the readers in Scotland and Canada who were to be exposed to Porter's trickery. If he had been alive in 1874 he would have been seventy two: it is therefore just possible that somebody drew his attention to Marcus Clarke's description of the seizure of the *Osprey* from Macquarie Harbour in the novel *For the Term of His Natural Life*. What would Porter have done as he realized that whole passages were borrowed from his own account published by Elliston thirty-six years earlier? He may well have smiled, for the net result is a Porter triumph. Clarke portrayed Porter as the least willing of the mutineers who manages to botch the most marginal of roles. In the pages of the most famous convict novel of them all, James Porter is guilty of being little more than a frightened dupe - but who nevertheless manages to make his escape. The long and short of it is that *For the Term of His Natural Life* contains yet another version of the Porter narrative, although in the pages of the novel Porter's words are attributed to the fictional John Rex. This version is introduced as follows: it is 1838 and Sylvia reads a manuscript *'written in a firm, large hand'*.

A NARRATIVE

Of the sufferings and adventures of the ten convicts who seized the brig Osprey at Macquarie Harbour in Van Diemens Land, related by one of the said convicts while lying under sentence for this offence in the gaol at Hobart Town.

In this version eight of the actual mutineers are named but Porter is not. Although present in the novel at the point when the *Osprey* is seized, thereafter Porter slips from the page. The other missing mutineer is John Dady, scratched to make way for the fictional John Rex. Porter is, however, an absent presence, for the words attributed to Rex are largely lifted from Porters's 1838 account. In the guise of John Rex, Porter stands innocent and manly on the shores of Botany Bay.

When James Porter disembarked from the *Asia* in 1824, he told the muster master that he was a *'beer machine maker'* by trade, and if the muster master batted an eye, the clerk at the desk simply wrote down what he was told. There was, of course, no such occupation. Brewing, though sometimes on a large scale, was not then mechanised, although the idea of a machine which magically manufactures beer has a certain appeal. You can hear the convict sniggers and guffaws, and what makes this joke complete is the play on his own name, Porter, the name of the dark ale for which London was then famous.

When the *Frederick* sailed off over the horizon, descriptions of the mutineers were drawn up and posted off to London. Armed with this script the Imperial authorities commenced their search for a *one-eyed beer machine maker*: Can you hear the roars of laughter?

Hamish Maxwell-Stewart

This afterword is an extract from *Seven Tales for a Man with Seven Sides*. The full text is published in *CHAIN LETTERS Narrating Convict Lives* by Lucy Frost and Hamish Maxwell-Stewart, Melbourne University Press 2001.

NOTES ON THE TEXT

3/   The date of birth is written clearly on Page One in the manuscript as 1807 but this does not correspond to any of Porter's other declarations of age: in 1818 he says he is 16 years old (see pp 7 & 9).

11/   *Fernando Martel.* Porter's memory for names is a little suspect. In the 1837 account of the seizure of the *Frederick* he names the Governor of Valdivia *Ferando Martel* - in this account named *Sanchez.*

11-12/   *Lord Cochrane.* Commander of the British Naval Squadron sent to aid the rebels against the Spanish. Porter's claims to be a *patriot* provide him with welcome leverage when he returns to Chile aboard the *Frederick.*

12/   *Gulliver.* The library available to prisoners at Norfolk Island may have contained a copy of the popular classic.

13/   This rather absurd description - in the manner of *back to back they faced each other* - may be part of Porter's cant humour, hinting that he may admit to greater culpability in the matter.

20/   *Whitesmith.* Generally refers to smiths working in metals other than iron - gold, silver, copper and tin. Porter's scam here was common, men admitting to skills they did not posses, or not acknowledging those they did. None of Porter's records show his skills as a sailor, and at one point he is recorded as illiterate.

23/   *Natives (Aborigines).* After nearly twenty years of relatively peaceful coexistence, the relationship between black and white in Van Diemens Land suffers under the pressure of an invasion by hundreds of thousands of sheep. The so-called Black Wars began.

24/   Not *Eaglehawk Neck* but from its description the narrows where now is the *Dunally Canal.*

31/   *The Commandant.* Captain James Briggs. Porter's account of the conditions at Macquarie Harbour are exaggerated: the *Small Island* held no more than 40 men; there were only 12 murders recorded in the whole 12 years of the Settlement; and a 96% punishment rate does not correspond to records of that period. The *suit of yellow* was not used at Macquarie Harbour.

33/   *Sugarloaf Mountain.* Probably the present Mount Sorrell, though why Porter would want to climb to the summit and then descend to the Phillip Island Camps is puzzling.

35/   On December 18th 1832 James Porter and James Sheedy are sentenced to 100 lashes for absconding. At this time the Commandant is not Briggs but Bailey. The loss of the Pilot, George Bowhill, and his crew also took place much earlier, in July 1830, well before Bailey arrived.

38/   *John Riley.* Not recorded as one of the mutineers. But a recorded mutineer, John Jones, takes Riley as a pseudonym in Chile.

40/ In the earlier version of the story Porter does not record what he sang. The version published in Ireland in 1844 had him singing Irish ballads and *Rule Britannia*, but it is most likely that *The Grand Conservation* featured: a soldiers' song expressing rebellious sentiments about working conditions, partcularly against austerity measures for the army introduced by the new King George IV: the *Sailor King* favoured the Navy.

43/ *George Williams*. Not recorded as a mutineer. Cheshire adopts William Williams as a pseudonym in Chile, and on p37 Porter notes that Cheshire worked as cook to John Barker!

44/ *Cap and Bonnet*. Two small islands about half a mile inside the entrance. The entrance at *Hells Gates* is barely 70 metres wide and the task of moving a ship out as Porter describes, with a fast ebb tide running, was often trickier than bringing her in.

51/ *Bueon*. The *Rio Bueno* just south of Valdivia.

56/ *The Government Mark,* popularly known as the *Convict Arrow*, was placed on all Government property, including prisoners' clothing, which helped to create that association.

65/ *James O'Connor*. The number of Irish names adopted may be explained with reference to the name of the Liberator of Chile - *Bernado O'Higgins*.

68/ *The Englishmen*. It is clear from this account that Porter was not himself present, being still up country at the Cider works.

76/ The three who managed to board the *Ocean* and escape were John Dady, John Fare and John Jones. They were never recaptured. Lesley, Barker and Russen were later reported free in Jamaica.

93/ *Catalina and Bernado*. Bernado named after the Chilean Liberator. William Shires remained in Australia after a pardon granted in 1845. His family reside in Darwin. His grandson was Sergeant Walter Shires, a pioneer aviator who made the first flight England to Australia in 1919 with Ross and Keith Smith.

95/ Porter's characterisation of Cheshire as an arch-villain may be a self-serving misrepresentation, creating a scapegoat to cover for his own machinations. Cheshire remained in Australia after gaining a pardon in 1846.

105/ Porter entirely fails to mention the appeal for clemency and the extraordinary arguments presented to Justice Pedder by William Shires in favour of quashing the guilty verdict: that they were guilty of no more than theft, having seized an unregistered vessel more properly described as *a quantity of wood and other materials so fastened as to possess the means of becoming a brig but having no one constituent necessary to justify those materials being then so called* ~ it was merely a floating bundle of wood.

THE LAST WORD

Some stories survive, not necessarily the great stories and if this is not a great story it is an intriguing one: apart from its appeal as an entertaining yarn, James Porter's tale touches us for a very simple reason. We know he is a rogue and a liar, we suspect he is self-serving and self promoting, even narcissistic, not to be trusted - a self-confessed trickster who nevertheless wants us to think the best of him. But beyond those irritations and failings, his simple and persistent desire, in the face of all setbacks, to be a free man speaks to us across two centuries of Australian experience:

> *The only place on this earth where we belong,*
> *where any of us belong,*
> *is where we can live as free men.*

Porter's story survives. I first heard the tale of the escape in 1981 and wrote a play about it. At the time of this reprint *The Round Earth Company* is approaching the 5000th performance at the Strahan Amphitheatre in Macquarie Harbour on Tasmania's West Coast of *The Ship That Never Was,* the story of the *Frederick* escapees, based on the narratives of James Porter: voyager, thief, felon, escapee, swashbuckler, romancer and writer of tales, who started his remarkable career because he wanted to go to the Theatre Royal in Drury Lane and did not have the price of a ticket.

Richard Innes Davey
Strahan 2003

Check out the cast members!